VOLU

OLD TES

M000287180

THE

NEW COLLEGEVILLE
BIBLE COMMENTARY

SONG OF SONGS
RUTH
LAMENTATIONS
ECCLESIASTES – ACTS.
ESTHER

Irene Nowell, O.S.B.

SERIES EDITOR
Daniel Durken, O.S.B.

LITURGICAL PRESS
Collegeville, Minnesota

www.litpress.org

Nihil Obstat: Reverend Robert Harren, *Censor deputatus*.
Imprimatur: ✠ Most Reverend John F. Kinney, J.C.D., D.D., Bishop of St. Cloud, Minnesota, June 24, 2013.

Design by Ann Blattner.

Cover illustration: Detail of *Ruth and Naomi* by Suzanne Moore. © 2010 *The Saint John's Bible*, Saint John's University, Collegeville, Minnesota. Used with permission. All rights reserved.

Photos: pages 15, 38, 67, 75, and 112, Thinkstock Photos.

Maps created by Robert Cronan of Lucidity Information Design, LLC.

1	2	3	4	5	6	7	8	9

Library of Congress Cataloging-in-Publication Data

Nowell, Irene, 1940–
    Song of Songs, Ruth, Lamentations, Ecclesiastes, Esther / Irene Nowell, O.S.B.
       pages cm. — (New Collegeville Bible commentary. Old Testament ; Volume 24)
    Includes index.
    ISBN 978-0-8146-2858-4 (alk. paper)
    1. Bible. Five Scrolls—Commentaries.　I. Title.
BS1309.N69　2013
221.7'7—dc23
2013013635

CONTENTS

Contents

ABBREVIATIONS

Books of the Bible

Acts—Acts of the Apostles
Amos—Amos
Bar—Baruch
1 Chr—1 Chronicles
2 Chr—2 Chronicles
Col—Colossians
1 Cor—1 Corinthians
2 Cor—2 Corinthians
Dan—Daniel
Deut—Deuteronomy
Eccl (or Qoh)—Ecclesiastes
Eph—Ephesians
Esth—Esther
Exod—Exodus
Ezek—Ezekiel
Ezra—Ezra
Gal—Galatians
Gen—Genesis
Hab—Habakkuk
Hag—Haggai
Heb—Hebrews
Hos—Hosea
Isa—Isaiah
Jas—James
Jdt—Judith
Jer—Jeremiah
Job—Job
Joel—Joel
John—John
1 John—1 John
2 John—2 John
3 John—3 John
Jonah—Jonah
Josh—Joshua
Jude—Jude
Judg—Judges
1 Kgs—1 Kings

2 Kgs—2 Kings
Lam—Lamentations
Lev—Leviticus
Luke—Luke
1 Macc—1 Maccabees
2 Macc—2 Maccabees
Mal—Malachi
Mark—Mark
Matt—Matthew
Mic—Micah
Nah—Nahum
Neh—Nehemiah
Num—Numbers
Obad—Obadiah
1 Pet—1 Peter
2 Pet—2 Peter
Phil—Philippians
Phlm—Philemon
Prov—Proverbs
Ps(s)—Psalms
Rev—Revelation
Rom—Romans
Ruth—Ruth
1 Sam—1 Samuel
2 Sam—2 Samuel
Sir—Sirach
Song—Song of Songs
1 Thess—1 Thessalonians
2 Thess—2 Thessalonians
1 Tim—1 Timothy
2 Tim—2 Timothy
Titus—Titus
Tob—Tobit
Wis—Wisdom
Zech—Zechariah
Zeph—Zephaniah

INTRODUCTION

The Festival Scrolls

Five Old Testament books are identified in the Hebrew Bible as the Festival Scrolls, or *Megilloth* (Hebrew: "scrolls"): Song of Songs, Ruth, Lamentations, Ecclesiastes (also known as Qoheleth), and Esther. These short books are read at important Jewish festivals during the year: The Song of Songs is read in the spring on Passover as a testimony of God's love for the chosen people. The book of Ruth is read on Pentecost (Weeks) because the date of this festival is set by counting the seven weeks between the beginning of the barley harvest and the beginning of the wheat harvest; the story of Ruth is set in that time frame. Lamentations is read in some Jewish communities on the ninth of Ab, the commemoration in late July or early August of the destruction of the temple in 587 B.C. and A.D. 70. Ecclesiastes is read on the feast of Booths, the last harvest festival of the year (September–October). The book of Esther provides the foundation for the celebration of Purim in the winter month of Adar (February–March).

These five books have a tangled history in Jewish and Christian Bibles. Jews debated into the first century A.D. whether Song of Songs, Ecclesiastes, and Esther belonged in the Scriptures at all. Esther is the only book of the Hebrew Scriptures that was not found among the Dead Sea Scrolls. The Hebrew version of Esther (see Introduction to Esther) and the Song of Songs are the only two biblical books that never mention God, which may be why they were questioned. All five books have been put in different places in different versions of Scripture. The Septuagint (the Greek translation of Jewish Scripture) placed Ruth where the story fits chronologically, between Judges and 1 Samuel, which is where it is found in Christian Bibles. In the Septuagint (followed again by Christian Bibles) Lamentations is found after Jeremiah, who was traditionally considered its author. All five books have always been included in the third section of the Hebrew Scriptures, called the Writings, where they are found in Jewish Bibles today. Even in the Writings, however, their arrangement has varied in different manuscripts. The Hebrew text used by scholars has an arrangement from the eleventh-century Leningrad manuscript: Ruth, Song of Songs, Ecclesiastes, Lamentations,

7

Esther. Hebrew Bibles used by most Jews today arrange the books in liturgical order as they are in this commentary. In Christian Bibles Esther is found with the historical books—after Tobit and Judith in the Roman Catholic canon and after Nehemiah in the Protestant canon. Ecclesiastes and Song of Songs are found after Proverbs among the wisdom books.

Despite their "wandering ways," each of these little books has a poetic beauty and a powerful message. Having them gathered in one small volume gives the reader a wealth of God's word to ponder.

Song of Songs

Title

"Song of Songs" is the Hebrew way of conveying the superlative: the best song (compare "king of kings" or "holy of holies"). The Song is attributed to Solomon. This attribution is more like a dedication than a declaration of authorship. The work is put under the patronage of Solomon, who is mentioned in it seven times (1:1, 5; 3:7, 9, 11; 8:11, 12). This dedication links the Song to the wisdom literature. The wisdom books Proverbs and Ecclesiastes are also dedicated to Solomon, who is said to have "uttered three thousand proverbs, and his songs numbered a thousand and five" (1 Kgs 5:12). Wisdom is based on common human experience and its goal is the good life. God is found in ordinary life. When the Song of Songs is read through a wisdom lens, it reveals the goodness of God in the experience of human love.

Genre and structure

The Song is a collection of love poetry, celebrating the joys and longings of human love. The songs are so skillfully woven together that there is no agreement on how many songs are collected or where each song begins and ends. Repeated phrases act as refrains, however, giving some indication of structure. Different voices, evident in the Hebrew verb forms, are marked in many translations: M = the man; W = the woman; D = Daughters of Jerusalem.

Poetic artistry

The Song is rich in poetic beauty, especially metaphorical expressions. The comparisons are from both nature and human achievement such as architecture. Themes common to love poetry, such as searching and finding, weave throughout. Repeated words and phrases bind the whole work together.

Date

The Song of Songs is difficult to date. Parts of the work undoubtedly circulated orally before the book was written. Analysis of the language suggests that the writing occurred sometime after the Babylonian exile, perhaps around the fourth century B.C.

Interpretation

Early in Jewish tradition the Song of Songs was interpreted as an allegory of the love between God and the covenant people. In Christian tradition too the Song was understood to describe the love between God and the church or the individual soul. This tradition of interpretation flourished in the Middle Ages, especially among the Cistercians. In recent times interpreters have returned to the original sense of the Song as a celebration of human love.

Song of Songs

1 ¹The Song of Songs, which is Solomon's.

The Woman Speaks of Her Lover

W ²Let him kiss me with kisses of
his mouth,
for your love is better than wine,
³better than the fragrance of
your perfumes.
Your name is a flowing perfume—
therefore young women love you.
⁴Draw me after you! Let us run!
The king has brought me to his
bed chambers.

Let us exult and rejoice in you;
let us celebrate your love: it is
beyond wine!
Rightly do they love you!

Love's Boast

W ⁵I am black and beautiful,
Daughters of Jerusalem—
Like the tents of Qedar,
like the curtains of Solomon.
⁶Do not stare at me because I am so
black,
because the sun has burned me.

A DECLARATION OF LOVE

Song of Songs 1:1-6

1:2-4 The woman speaks of her lover

After the title (1:1, see Introduction), the Song begins with the woman's passionate outcry of love. She speaks to her lover and about him in the same breath. He is eminently desirable and his love is intoxicating. The sound of his name fills her with sweetness. (In Hebrew "name" is *shem* and "perfume" is *shemen*.) She is certain that every woman loves him!

1:5-6 Love's boast

The woman's description of herself inserts a note of tension. She speaks to the "Daughters of Jerusalem," a group that functions as a chorus through-out the Song (2:7; 3:5, 10; 5:8, 16; 8:4). She is black and beautiful. The wom-an's color is compared to the desert tents made of black goat hair and to curtains either of Solomon's own tent or of Solomon's temple. The wealthy tribe of Qedar (a word which means "dark") lived in the Arabian Peninsula and is associated with Ishmael (see Gen 25:13; Isa 60:7), so "black" here

11

The sons of my mother were angry
with me;
they charged me with the care of
the vineyards:
my own vineyard I did not take
care of.

Love's Inquiry

◀ W ⁷Tell me, you whom my soul loves,
where you shepherd, where you
give rest at midday.
Why should I be like one wandering
after the flocks of your
companions?

M ⁸If you do not know,
most beautiful among women,
Follow the tracks of the flock
and pasture your lambs
near the shepherds' tents.

Love's Vision

M ⁹To a mare among Pharaoh's
chariotry
I compare you, my friend:
¹⁰Your cheeks lovely in pendants,
your neck in jewels.
¹¹We will make pendants of gold for
you,
and ornaments of silver.

suggests beauty and luxury. But the woman's blackness came at a price. She has been forced by her brothers to work outdoors and the sun has burned her. What does the "vineyard" mean? Her sun-blackened skin indicates work in a literal vineyard. Throughout the Song, however, the vineyard also symbolizes the woman herself, her beauty and fertility (see 8:12) and the love between the man and the woman (see 2:15; 7:13).

A CONVERSATION BETWEEN THE LOVERS

Song of Songs 1:7–2:7

1:7-8 Love's inquiry

Now the woman begins a conversation with her lover. She will seek him at the time of the midday rest. She names him "you whom my soul loves," a phrase that becomes a refrain in 3:1-4 where the theme of seeking is intensified. The agricultural metaphors continue. She cared for the vineyards; they both are shepherds.

1:9-11 Love's vision

A dialogue of mutual admiration ensues. In this first speech the man compares the woman to a mare among pharaoh's chariotry. Comparison to a beautiful horse is a great compliment in the worldview of the Song. She is adorned with precious jewelry like the trappings of a horse. In addition, a mare turned loose among the chariot horses—all stallions—would cause chaos. Her beauty, her strength, and her desirability are all praised in this metaphor.

▶ This symbol indicates a cross reference number in the *Catechism of the Catholic Church*. See page 142 for number citations.

How Near Is Love!

W ¹²While the king was upon his
    couch,
    my spikenard gave forth its
        fragrance.
  ¹³My lover is to me a sachet of
    myrrh;
    between my breasts he lies.
  ¹⁴My lover is to me a cluster of
    henna
    from the vineyards of En-gedi.
M ¹⁵How beautiful you are, my friend,
    how beautiful! your eyes are
        doves!
W ¹⁶How beautiful you are, my lover—
    handsome indeed!
  Verdant indeed is our couch;
    ¹⁷the beams of our house are
        cedars,
    our rafters, cypresses.
2 W ¹I am a flower of Sharon,
    a lily of the valleys.

M ²Like a lily among thorns,
    so is my friend among women.
W ³Like an apple tree among the trees
    of the woods,
    so is my lover among men.
In his shadow I delight to sit,
    and his fruit is sweet to my
        taste.
⁴He brought me to the banquet hall
    and his glance at me signaled
        love.
⁵Strengthen me with raisin cakes,
    refresh me with apples,
    for I am sick with love.
⁶His left hand is under my head
    and his right arm embraces me.
⁷I adjure you, Daughters of
    Jerusalem,
    by the gazelles and the does of
        the field,
Do not awaken, or stir up love
    until it is ready.

1:12–2:7 Love's union

The woman returns to the subject of sweet smells (1:12-14; see 1:3). In her longing for him she gives off the sweet scent of spikenard, an aromatic herb from India used in making ointments. This is probably the ointment used in the various anointings of Jesus (see Mark 14:3; John 12:3). The man is a cluster of fragrant spices lying between her breasts. Myrrh is a sweet-smelling gum resin from various trees of Arabia and India. Henna is a shrub of the loosestrife family that has fragrant white or reddish flowers. Spices were valuable in the ancient world for fragrance, flavoring, and as an embalming agent. Stores of spices were a sign of wealth (see 2 Kgs 20:13).

The two lovers exchange compliments: "How beautiful you are" (1:15-16). He calls her "my friend." The feminine form of this word occurs nine times in the Song and only one other time in the Hebrew Bible (Judg 11:37). She calls him "my lover," a term she uses twenty-six times. He again uses a visual metaphor: her eyes are like doves. Soft, gentle, gray-brown? She responds with a metaphor of fragrance: their house is made of sweet-smelling wood. Inside a building or in a grove of trees?

The conversation between the man and the woman continues (2:1-3), building on the plant metaphors of chapter one. She compares herself

Her Lover's Visit Remembered

W   ⁸The sound of my lover! here he
          comes
        springing across the mountains,
        leaping across the hills.
     ⁹My lover is like a gazelle
        or a young stag.
    See! He is standing behind our wall,
        gazing through the windows,
        peering through the lattices.
     ¹⁰My lover speaks and says to me,
M   "Arise, my friend, my beautiful
          one,
        and come!

¹¹For see, the winter is past,
    the rains are over and gone.
¹²The flowers appear on the earth,
    the time of pruning the vines
        has come,
    and the song of the turtledove is
        heard in our land.
¹³The fig tree puts forth its figs,
    and the vines, in bloom, give
        forth fragrance.
Arise, my friend, my beautiful one,
    and come!
¹⁴My dove in the clefts of the rock,
    in the secret recesses of the cliff,

---

to the first flowers of spring: the crocus or narcissus growing on the fertile coastal Plain of Sharon and the lotus flower (a lily) growing in the valleys. He emphasizes her uniqueness, "a lily among thorns." She responds with her own metaphor of his uniqueness. He is a fruit-bearing tree among the other trees of the wood. This tree is not our common apple tree, which is not native to Israel, but an undomesticated fruit tree. She proclaims her lover the bearer of sweet fruit and the giver of pleasant shade. These images lead to metaphors of eating and finally a direct statement of love. He brings her to the place of eating, the place of love. She is weak with passion and longing. He takes her in his embrace.

The final verse in this section (2:7) is a refrain that occurs several times in the Song. The woman puts the Daughters under oath not to arouse love until it is ready. Is this a plea not to disturb the two lovers? Or is it advice that genuine love has its own time and we must wait for it? The oath—"by the gazelles and the does of the field"—is a euphemism for names of God. The Hebrew words for "gazelles" and "does" (*tsebaoth, ayeloth*) sound like the words for "hosts" in the term "Lord of hosts" (*tsebaoth*) and for "God" (*eyl* or *eloah*). This is similar to our use of "gosh" for "God" or "jeepers creepers" for "Jesus Christ."

HER LOVER'S VISIT REMEMBERED

Song of Songs 2:8-17

This section is a passionate description of the delight of lovers in springtime. The song is beautifully structured. It is linked to the previous song by the images of gazelle and deer (2:7, 9). The end of the song echoes its

"For see, the winter is past, the rains are over and gone. The flowers appear on the earth . . ." (Song 2:11-12).

Let me see your face,
　　let me hear your voice,
For your voice is sweet,
　　and your face is lovely."
W [15]Catch us the foxes, the little foxes
　　that damage the vineyards; for
　　　　our vineyards are in
　　　　bloom!

[16]My lover belongs to me and I to
　　him;
　　he feeds among the lilies.
[17]Until the day grows cool and the
　　shadows flee,
　　roam, my lover,
Like a gazelle or a young stag
　　upon the rugged mountains.

---

beginning, forming what is known as an "inclusion." In verse 8 the lover arrives and in verse 17 he departs. He moves with the grace and speed of a gazelle or young stag (2:9, 17). An inner inclusion surrounds the description of the approaching spring; the phrase "Arise, my friend" is found in verses 10 and 13. The whole section is characterized by abundant images of sound, smell, sight, and anticipated taste. The verbs of springing and leaping, as well as the description of spring's rapid arrival, convey a sense of urgency.

The woman hears her lover's voice and sees him eagerly rushing toward her, but she stays hidden and forces him to search for her (2:8-9). He calls out to her with his favorite terms of endearment, "friend" and "beautiful one." He insists that she come out to enjoy the wonders of springtime (2:10). Spring is announced by the end of the rainy season, March or April in Israel, and the arrival of the first migrating birds. Vinedressers know that the grape vines must be pruned promptly, before the sap begins to rise. The description of spring appeals to all our senses. We feel the end of the winter rains; we see the flowers and the birds. We hear the doves cooing and anticipate the taste of grapes and figs (2:11-13).

The man continues his invitation to the woman, pleading with her to come out of hiding (2:14). He has compared her previously to a mare; now he compares her to a dove, a symbol of gentleness and love. The poetry of this verse is carefully worked, with the last four lines in a mirroring pattern: face, voice, voice, face. The woman answers with what may be a line of a song (2:15). The little foxes symbolize the other young men who would like to court her (the vineyard). She is warning her lover to pay attention to her. She continues with a declaration of her commitment (2:16) and an invitation to him to spend time with her, either the whole day or the whole night (2:17). It is difficult to tell whether the time she indicates is the evening, with its cool breezes, or the morning, when the shadows flee.

3 Loss and Discovery

W ¹On my bed at night I sought him
  whom my soul loves—
I sought him but I did not find him.
²"Let me rise then and go about the
    city,
  through the streets and squares;
Let me seek him whom my soul
    loves."
  I sought him but I did not find
    him.
³The watchmen found me,
  as they made their rounds in the
    city:
  "Him whom my soul loves—
    have you seen him?"

⁴Hardly had I left them
  when I found him whom my
    soul loves.
I held him and would not let him go
  until I had brought him to my
    mother's house,
to the chamber of her who
    conceived me.
⁵I adjure you, Daughters of
    Jerusalem,
  by the gazelles and the does of
    the field,
Do not awaken or stir up love
  until it is ready.

LOSS AND DISCOVERY

Song of Songs 3:1-5

The scene shifts to the woman's bedroom. She is alone and longing for her lover. The interweaving of repeated words and phrases carries the meaning of this scene: "seek/sought" (twice each in 3:1-2); "whom my soul loves" (3:1, 2, 3, 4); "not find/found" (3:1, 2, 3, 4); "go about/make rounds of the city" (3:2, 3). These repetitions make up over half the Hebrew words in verses 1-4 (26 of 50).

The woman's searching begins on her bed (3:1). Is this a dream? Or is her longing so intense that she gets up and goes out alone at night (3:2), an action uncharacteristic of women in that society? She seeks him but does not find him. Ironically, however, the watchmen find her! She is making her rounds of the city and so are they (3:2-3). She seeks "him whom [her] soul loves." This phrase identified her lover already in 1:7. Her love is so intense that she repeats this name for him four times. When she talks to the watchmen, she puts this phrase first: "Him whom my soul loves—have you seen him?"

Finally, when she finds him, new phrases appear (3:4-5). She clings to him and brings him to her mother's house (see also 8:2). The designation, "mother's house," is rare, occurring only twice more in the Old Testament, both times in stories of women and in the context of marriage (Gen 24:28, concerning Rebekah, and Ruth 1:8). She brings him to the room of her mother (literally, "the one who conceived her"). The passage begins and ends with the suggestion of a bed. The section ends with a repetition of the refrain of 2:7.

Solomon's Wedding Procession

D ⁶Who is this coming up from the desert,
   like columns of smoke
Perfumed with myrrh and frankincense,
   with all kinds of exotic powders?
⁷See! it is the litter of Solomon;
   sixty valiant men surround it,
   of the valiant men of Israel:
⁸All of them expert with the sword,
   skilled in battle,
Each with his sword at his side
   against the terrors of the night.

⁹King Solomon made himself an enclosed litter
   of wood from Lebanon.
¹⁰He made its columns of silver,
   its roof of gold,
Its seat of purple cloth,
   its interior lovingly fitted.
Daughters of Jerusalem, ¹¹go out
   and look upon King Solomon
In the crown with which his mother
   has crowned him
   on the day of his marriage,
   on the day of the joy of his heart.

SOLOMON'S WEDDING PROCESSION

Song of Songs 3:6-11

Not only does this poem begin with a question, there are questions about it. Who or what is this coming from the desert? It seems to be Solomon, coming to his wedding, although another opinion is that the one arriving is the bride. A further dispute concerns the number of pieces of furniture: is the litter in verses 7-8 the same as the one in verses 9-10? The NABRE translation suggests it is the same single piece of furniture.

The procession from the desert suggests the arrival of a caravan of merchants with all their exotic wares (3:6). The columns of smoke in the desert suggest also the exodus journey (see Exod 13:21-22). Both images reveal the elegance of this procession. The identification of the traveler as Solomon also enhances the vision (see Introduction). Throughout the Song the lovers are compared to a royal couple (see 1:4; 8:11-12). The number of warriors is double the usual guard (see Judg 14:11; 2 Sam 23:18-23). They are prepared to defend the lovers against any danger (3:7-8).

Solomon's litter is made of precious materials: cedar of Lebanon, gold and silver (3:9-10). Purple cloth was a sign of royalty because purple (or blue) dye, obtained from the murex shellfish, was very difficult to process. The framework or interior of the carriage is "lovingly fitted" (literally: "inlaid with love"), another indication of the impending union of the lovers. The witnesses to the wedding will be the Daughters of Jerusalem, so often summoned by the woman (see 1:5). The groom will be crowned by his mother with the wedding wreath (3:11). This is the only mention of marriage in the Song of Songs.

4 **The Beauty of the Woman**

M ¹How beautiful you are, my
    friend,
    how beautiful you are!
Your eyes are doves
    behind your veil.
Your hair is like a flock of goats
    streaming down Mount Gilead.
²Your teeth are like a flock of ewes
    to be shorn,
    that come up from the washing,
All of them big with twins,
    none of them barren.

³Like a scarlet strand
    and your mouth–
Like pomegranate hal
    cheeks
    behind your veil.
⁴Like a tower of David,) ᵤₓ neck,
    built in courses,
A thousand shields hanging upon
    it,
    all the armor of warriors.
⁵Your breasts are like two fawns,
    twins of a gazelle
    feeding among the lilies.

THE BEAUTY OF THE WOMAN

Song of Songs 4:1-11

The next section begins with a poem in praise of the beloved's physical beauty. The style is that of the Arabic *wasf*, a love song that compares parts of the beloved's body (top to bottom or the reverse) to images in nature or human art. Here the song is set off by an inclusion—"beautiful you are, my friend"—in verses 1 and 7. The man declares that everything about the woman is beautiful, even though he will only describe her from head to breasts.

A second inclusion, "behind your veil," sets off the description of her head (4:1-3). She is tantalizingly hidden, but this is a hiddenness that enhances rather than conceals her beauty. Her hair is like a flock of goats streaming down the mountain. The movement of the black goats, leaping downward, suggests long, wavy black hair. In contrast, her teeth are white as newly washed sheep and no teeth are missing. Her cheek is like a plump, red pomegranate. The man's gaze moves down to her neck adorned with many necklaces and pendants, which he compares to a strong, straight tower hung with the small round shields of victorious warriors (v. 4). Finally, her breasts are as soft and beautiful as young gazelles (4:5). Both the pomegranate with its many seeds and the gazelle, drinking from the stream that waters the tree of life, are ancient Near Eastern symbols of fertility. The man concludes his description by accepting the woman's invitation to come to the fragrant mountains (her breasts?) as the day grows cool and the shadows lengthen (4:6; see 2:17).

The lover's longing is evident in his insistent call to her to come to him (4:8). She seems as inaccessible as the mountain range of Lebanon with its

⁶Until the day grows cool
and the shadows flee,
I shall go to the mountain of
myrrh,
to the hill of frankincense.
⁷You are beautiful in every way, my
friend,
there is no flaw in you!
⁸With me from Lebanon, my bride!
With me from Lebanon, come!
Descend from the peak of Amana,
from the peak of Senir and
Hermon,
From the lairs of lions,
from the leopards' heights.
⁹ You have ravished my heart, my
sister, my bride;
you have ravished my heart
with one glance of your
eyes,
with one bead of your necklace.
¹⁰How beautiful is your love,
my sister, my bride,

How much better is your love than
wine,
and the fragrance of your
perfumes than any spice!
¹¹Your lips drip honey, my bride,
honey and milk are under your
tongue;
And the fragrance of your
garments
is like the fragrance of Lebanon.

The Lover's Garden

M ¹²A garden enclosed, my sister, my
bride,
a garden enclosed, a fountain
sealed!
¹³Your branches are a grove of
pomegranates,
with fruits of choicest yield:
Henna with spikenard,
¹⁴spikenard and saffron,
Sweet cane and cinnamon,
with all kinds of frankincense;

peaks of Hermon (called Senir by the Amorites, see Deut 3:9) and Amana (probably near Damascus, see 2 Kgs 5:12). She is as impossible to reach as if she were hidden in a wild animal's lair. The man now describes the effect of her beauty on him (4:9-11). He calls her "my sister," a frequent term of endearment for a wife (see Tob 5:21; 7:15; 8:4; 10:6), and "bride," a term that appears in the Song only in 4:9–5:1. He returns her praise of his love and fragrance (see 1:2-3). Her kisses are as sweet as honey and as nourishing as milk, images that recall the wonders of the Promised Land (see Exod 3:8, 17). Two kinds of "honey" are mentioned here: the first is domesticated honey, dripping or strained from the comb; the second is wild honey or the syrup from grapes or dates. Her fragrance is like Lebanon, either the famous cedars or frankincense (Hebrew, *lebonah*, see 4:6).

THE LOVER'S GARDEN

Song of Songs 4:12–5:1

The man continues his praise by describing the woman as an enclosed garden, a sealed fountain, reserved for him alone. The garden suggests Eden, and the term for "grove" in verse 13 is a Persian loanword, *pardes,*

Myrrh and aloes,
with all the finest spices;
¹⁵A garden fountain, a well of living
water,
streams flowing from Lebanon.
¹⁶Awake, north wind!
Come, south wind!
Blow upon my garden
that its perfumes may spread
abroad.
W Let my lover come to his garden
and eat its fruits of choicest
yield.
5 M ¹I have come to my garden,
my sister, my bride;
I gather my myrrh with my
spices,
I eat my honeycomb with my
honey,
I drink my wine with my milk.
D? Eat, friends; drink!
Drink deeply, lovers!

A Fruitless Search

W ²I was sleeping, but my heart was
awake.
The sound of my lover
knocking!

"Open to me, my sister, my friend,
my dove, my perfect one!
For my head is wet with dew,
my hair, with the moisture of
the night."
³I have taken off my robe,
am I then to put it on?
I have bathed my feet,
am I then to soil them?
⁴My lover put his hand in through
the opening:
my innermost being trembled
because of him.
⁵I rose to open for my lover,
my hands dripping myrrh:
My fingers, flowing myrrh
upon the handles of the lock.
⁶I opened for my lover—
but my lover had turned and
gone!
At his leaving, my soul sank.
I sought him, but I did not find
him;
I called out after him, but he did
not answer me.
⁷The watchmen found me,
as they made their rounds in the
city;

---

from which we get the word "paradise." She is truly an extraordinary garden in which all sorts of wonderful fruits and spices grow, precious items that in ordinary life must be imported from far and wide (4:13-14). Not only is she a watered garden, she is living water, flowing from the mountains of Lebanon (4:15). The man calls all the winds to spread the intoxicating fragrance of his garden; the woman interrupts with an invitation to him to come enjoy his garden (4:16). He replies that he has indeed come. The narrator encourages the lovers to enjoy their lovemaking (5:1).

A FRUITLESS SEARCH

Song of Songs 5:2-8

This section seems to be a replay of 3:1-5. Many of the images and phrases are the same, but the differences are significant. In 3:1 the woman was on her bed; in 5:2 she is not only on her bed, but sleeping. Yet, she says, her heart—

21

They beat me, they wounded me,
   they tore off my mantle,
   the watchmen of the walls.
⁸I adjure you, Daughters of
      Jerusalem,
   if you find my lover
What shall you tell him?
   that I am sick with love.

The Lost Lover Described

D ⁹How does your lover differ from
      any other lover,
      most beautiful among women?
How does your lover differ from
      any other,
   that you adjure us so?

---

the seat of both thought and emotion—is awake. Is she dreaming? Is she simply dozing? In any case, the vigorous knocking of her beloved interrupts her. He calls to her with four terms of endearment. Three have appeared before; the fourth, meaning "perfect" or "whole," suggests his description of her as altogether beautiful (4:1, 7). In chapter 3 she could not find him, but here he is! Both sides of their conversation seem self-centered. He is wet and she is ready for bed (5:2-3). The rendezvous will not happen.

The description of their encounter is filled with sexual innuendo. He asks her to open to him; she replies that she is naked and has bathed her feet (a common Hebrew euphemism for genitals). He puts his hand through the opening (the keyhole?) and her "innermost being" (literally: "innards") are in turmoil (5:4). But the desire of the lovers is not to be satisfied. By the time she rises to open for him, he is gone. The door, however, is dripping with myrrh (5:5). Has he left the perfume as a gift? Is this further innuendo?

At his departure her heart sinks and she goes in search of him. The phrases of 3:1-3 are repeated but each with an addition. Now she not only seeks him, she calls out after him (5:6, see 3:1-2). The watchmen not only find her, but they also beat her and strip her of her mantle (5:7, see: 3:3). She adjures the Daughters of Jerusalem, but her request is now that they tell her beloved that she is lovesick (5:8, see 2:5; 3:5). In every instance the description of her longing is intensified.

THE LOVER LOST AND FOUND

Song of Songs 5:9–6:3

Two questions from the Daughters of Jerusalem and the woman's answers structure this section. The Daughters ask how her lover is better than others (5:9) and where he has gone (6:1). Both times they address her with a title given her by the man: "most beautiful among women" (see 1:8). The woman's answer to the first question is a *wasf* about her lover's physical beauty. In her answer to the second she returns to the image of the garden (see 4:12-16).

W ¹⁰My lover is radiant and ruddy;
    outstanding among thousands.
¹¹His head is gold, pure gold,
    his hair like palm fronds,
    as black as a raven.
¹²His eyes are like doves
    beside streams of water,
Bathing in milk,
    sitting by brimming pools.
¹³His cheeks are like beds of spices
    yielding aromatic scents;
his lips are lilies
    that drip flowing myrrh.
¹⁴His arms are rods of gold
    adorned with gems;
His loins, a work of ivory
    covered with sapphires.
¹⁵His legs, pillars of alabaster,
    resting on golden pedestals.
His appearance, like the Lebanon,
    imposing as the cedars.
¹⁶His mouth is sweetness itself;
    he is delightful in every way.
Such is my lover, and such my
    friend,
    Daughters of Jerusalem!

The Lost Lover Found

6 D ¹Where has your lover gone,
    most beautiful among women?
Where has your lover withdrawn
    that we may seek him with you?
W ²My lover has come down to his
    garden,
    to the beds of spices,
To feed in the gardens
    and to gather lilies.
³I belong to my lover, and my lover
    belongs to me;
    he feeds among the lilies.

5:9-16 The lost lover described

The woman describes her lover much as he described her. She moves from head to foot and concludes with praise of his mouth (see 4:11). She begins and ends by emphasizing his complete desirability (5:10, 16; see 4:1, 7). The images differ, however. He used two terms for honey in describing her mouth; she uses two terms for gold in describing his head. (A third term describes his golden feet!) His hair is thick and luxuriant, like branches of the date palm or clusters of fruit (5:11). His eyes too are like doves (see 1:15; 4:1) bathed in milk (i.e., not bloodshot). His cheeks and lips are fragrant and intoxicating (5:13).

As she moves to a description of his torso, the imagery shifts, suggesting the statue of a god. He is made of precious metals set with gemstones (5:14-15). He is as impressive as the cedars of Lebanon. He can be compared to the statue of Nebuchadnezzar (Dan 2:31-34), but unlike Nebuchadnezzar, he does not have clay feet. He is utterly desirable (5:16).

6:1-3 The lost lover found

The Daughters' second question suggests that the woman ought to know where this marvelous man has gone. Perhaps the Daughters would like to find him too (6:1). The woman's response makes it clear that he belongs to her alone. He has come to her, his enclosed garden (6:2; see 4:12-15). The section ends with the statement of mutual possession (6:3; see 2:16).

The Beauty of the Woman

M ⁴Beautiful as Tirzah are you,
my friend;
fair as Jerusalem,
fearsome as celestial visions!
⁵Turn your eyes away from me,
for they stir me up.
Your hair is like a flock of goats
streaming down from Gilead.
⁶Your teeth are like a flock of ewes
that come up from the washing,
All of them big with twins,
none of them barren.
⁷Like pomegranate halves,
your cheeks behind your veil.

⁸Sixty are the queens, eighty the
concubines,
and young women without
number—
⁹One alone is my dove, my perfect
one,
her mother's special one,
favorite of the one who bore her.
Daughters see her and call her happy,
queens and concubines, and
they praise her:
¹⁰"Who is this that comes forth like
the dawn,
beautiful as the white moon,
pure as the blazing sun,
fearsome as celestial visions?"

THE BEAUTY OF THE WOMAN

Song of Songs 6:4-10

The lover has returned and repeats much of a previous *wasf* in praise of the woman (compare 4:1-3 to 6:5-7) with some differences. The woman's eyes, like doves, which ravished his heart (4:9), have become even more exciting (6:5). His beautiful, perfect one (4:7) is better than any other woman; even queens sing her praises (6:9).

Just as the *wasf* in 4:1-7 was surrounded by an inclusion, declaring the perfect beauty of the beloved, so this *wasf* is enclosed ("beautiful" and "fearsome" in 6:4, 10). In 4:4 the man compared the woman's bejeweled neck to David's tower. Now he compares his beloved to two capital cities: Tirzah, capital city of the northern kingdom (Israel) from 910–870 B.C., and Jerusalem, capital city of the southern kingdom (Judah). Although Samaria is the best known of Israel's three capital cities, Tirzah may have been chosen because its root word means "to be pleased with." The repetition of the inclusion (6:10) does not compare the woman to cities but to cosmic realities. She is as beautiful as the moon, literally "the white," referring to the full moon; as pure as the sun, literally "the heat." These comparisons reach toward the divine, since sun and moon were sometimes considered gods in the ancient Near East.

The last phrase of the inclusion is difficult to translate. The woman is as fearsome as what? The last word, which occurs only here in the Old Testament, comes from a root meaning "banners," "signals," or "divisions." It has often been interpreted in a military context as "bannered troops."

Love's Meeting	The Beauty of the Beloved
W ¹¹To the walnut grove I went down, to see the young growth of the valley; To see if the vines were in bloom, if the pomegranates had blossomed. ¹²Before I knew it, my desire had made me the blessed one of the prince's people.	7 D? ¹Turn, turn, O Shulammite! turn, turn that we may gaze upon you! W How can you gaze upon the Shulammite as at the dance of the two camps? M ²How beautiful are your feet in sandals, O noble daughter!

But in this context, with the sun and the moon, it may mean the stars, the armies (hosts) of heaven, thus "celestial visions."

LOVE'S MEETING

Song of Songs 6:11-12

It is not clear who is speaking in these verses. Previously the man came down to the garden (5:1; 6:2), which symbolized the woman (4:12-16). Here, however, the woman seems to be speaking. She goes down to enjoy the new growth of springtime. On the eastern end of the Mediterranean as soon as the rains stop there is an explosion of blossoms, flowering trees, and wildflowers. The vision overwhelms the woman.

THE BEAUTY OF THE BELOVED

Song of Songs 7:1-6

A third *wasf* about the woman (see 4:1-7; 6:4-10) is introduced by a mysterious verse addressed (apparently by the Daughters) to the "Shulammite" (i.e., the woman). The name "Shulammite" is unknown. It may be another spelling for "Shunammite," a woman from Shunem, a city in Galilee. Abishag, the last concubine of David, was a Shunammite (1 Kgs 1–2), as was the friend and benefactor of Elisha (2 Kgs 4). It may be a feminized form of Solomon (*shelomo* in Hebrew), indicating that the woman has royal status (see 7:2), or it may simply be derived from *shalom*, peace.

The woman is commanded to "turn" so that she may be seen, presumably because of her beauty (7:1). Her response indicates that they are watching her dance. The dance, otherwise unknown, is called "the dance of the two camps."

This third *wasf* sung by the man is the most explicitly erotic. The direction of his gaze from foot to head is the reversal of the other two. He begins

Your curving thighs like jewels,
the product of skilled hands.
³Your valley, a round bowl
that should never lack mixed
wine.
Your belly, a mound of wheat,
encircled with lilies.
⁴Your breasts are like two fawns,
twins of a gazelle.
⁵Your neck like a tower of ivory;
your eyes, pools in Heshbon
by the gate of Bath-rabbim.
Your nose like the tower of Lebanon
that looks toward Damascus.
⁶Your head rises upon you like
Carmel;
your hair is like purple;
a king is caught in its locks.

Love's Desires

⁷How beautiful you are, how fair,
my love, daughter of delights!
⁸Your very form resembles a
date-palm,
and your breasts, clusters.
⁹I thought, "Let me climb the
date-palm!
Let me take hold of its branches!
Let your breasts be like clusters of
the vine
and the fragrance of your breath
like apples,
¹⁰And your mouth like the best
wine—

W   that flows down smoothly for
my lover,
gliding over my lips and teeth.

with her feet, enticingly shod in sandals (see Jdt 10:4; 16:9). The word used here for "feet" refers to the beat of her steps (in the dance?). He moves upward to her thighs, her navel, her belly, describing her full roundness with symbols of richness and fertility (6:2-3). He again compares her breasts to the twins of a gazelle and her neck to a tower, but now the tower is precious ivory (6:4-5; see 4:4-5). Her nose is a tower too. We may not think that is a compliment, but Lebanon suggests the white moon (Hebrew *lebanah*, see 6:10) or white, sweet-smelling frankincense (*lebonah*). Damascus is the prosperous and powerful capital city of Aram (Syria); Heshbon, in Moab, was the capital city of Sihon, king of the Amorites. The two cities lie on the northern and southern ends of the Kings' Highway. This woman's face—eyes and nose—are as strong and compelling as cities on the caravan route. (Bath-rabbim is unknown, perhaps Rabbah, just north of Heshbon.) Finally, the woman's head is as commanding as Mt. Carmel, rising over the Mediterranean; her blue-black hair, precious as royal purple, captivates her king (7:6). His praise recognizes the strength of this woman.

LOVE'S DESIRES

Song of Songs 7:7–8:4

The man again exclaims over the woman's beauty (see 1:15-16; 4:1, 7) and desires to enjoy it. Her stature is that of a palm tree with its clusters of dates high and out of reach, but her inaccessibility will not be a barrier to

¹¹I belong to my lover,
    his yearning is for me.
¹²Come, my lover! Let us go out to
    the fields,
    let us pass the night among the
    henna.
¹³Let us go early to the vineyards,
    and see
    if the vines are in bloom,
If the buds have opened,
    if the pomegranates have
    blossomed;
There will I give you my love.
¹⁴The mandrakes give forth
    fragrance,
    and over our doors are all choice
    fruits;
Fruits both fresh and dried, my
    lover,
    have I kept in store for you.

8 ¹Would that you were a brother
    to me,
    nursed at my mother's breasts!
If I met you out of doors, I would
    kiss you

and none would despise me.
²I would lead you, bring you to my
    mother's house,
    where you would teach me,
Where I would give you to drink
    spiced wine, my pomegranate
    juice.
³His left hand is under my head,
    and his right arm embraces me.
⁴I adjure you, Daughters of
    Jerusalem,
    do not awaken or stir up love
    until it is ready!

The Return from the Desert

D? ⁵Who is this coming up from the
    desert,
    leaning upon her lover?
W Beneath the apple tree I awakened
    you;
    there your mother conceived
    you;
    there she who bore you
    conceived.

---

him. Once more he begins to compare her to delicious fruits—dates, apples, grapes and their wine—but she interrupts him, offering herself (7:8-10). She reverses the statement in Genesis, where the woman is told, "*your* urge shall be for your husband" (Gen 3:16; emphasis added). This woman declares that her *lover's* yearning is for her (7:11). With images reminiscent of her visit to the nut garden (6:11), she invites him to come with her into the fields for lovemaking (7:12-13). The mandrake, an herb called *duda'im* in Hebrew (compare *dodi*, "beloved"), was considered an aphrodisiac because of its human-like shape (7:14). Rachel, longing for a child, bargained with Leah for mandrakes (Gen 30:14-16). This woman has treasured up all her fruitfulness for her lover.

    The woman wishes the man were her brother so that she could show her affection without scandalizing others (8:1). This is different from the affectionate term, "sister," used by the man (see 4:9-10, 12; 5:1, 2); this is a wish for sibling relationship. Again she wants to bring him to her mother's house (see 3:4). The drinks she will give him suggest the intoxication of love. Also the Hebrew word for "drink" in verse 2 (*shaqah*) echoes the word

27

True Love

⁶Set me as a seal upon your heart,
 as a seal upon your arm;
For Love is strong as Death,
 longing is fierce as Sheol.
Its arrows are arrows of fire,

flames of the divine.
⁷Deep waters cannot quench love,
 nor rivers sweep it away.
Were one to offer all the wealth of
 his house for love,
 he would be utterly despised.

---

for "kiss" (*nashaq*) in verse 1. An almost verbatim repetition of earlier verses closes the unit (2:6-7; see 3:5).

REPRISE

Song of Songs 8:5-14

8:5 The return from the desert

The last ten verses of the Song of Songs are like a reprise of all the melodies heard throughout the work. The echo of "Who is this coming" appears here (see 3:6; 6:10). In chapter 3 we saw the litter of Solomon coming in a cloud of perfume; here it is the woman leaning on her lover. At the end of the same passage, his mother crowned him with the wedding wreath (3:11). This scene is set under the tree where his mother conceived him. The woman has compared her lover to an apple tree and delighted to rest in his shadow (2:3); she has asked the Daughters of Jerusalem not to arouse love before its time (2:7; 3:5; 8:4). Now she declares that she has aroused her lover under the apple tree.

8:6-7 True love

The most powerful statement of love in the Song is at the center of chapter 8. The seal is a sign of identity. It may be a cylinder seal worn around the neck or a scarab ring worn on the finger. Whoever sees the seal or its imprint recognizes the owner, just as a signature is used as identification today. She declares that she is as bound to him as his own identity. Love is as impossible to stop as death; passion is as devouring as Sheol, the home of the dead. Even chaos cannot sweep it away, nor is there anything that can buy it.

The nouns here suggest the names of Canaanite gods: Mot (Death), Resheph (translated "flames," the name of the god of pestilence, often portrayed with arrows), and Yamm (sea, or the waters of chaos). The name of Israel's god is suggested at the end of verse 6, which ends with Yah, a short form of Y<small>HWH</small>. The phrase may mean "flames of Y<small>HWH</small>" or "flames as powerful as a god."

An Answer to the Brothers

W ⁸"We have a little sister;
　　she has no breasts as yet.
What shall we do for our sister
　　on the day she is spoken for?
⁹If she is a wall,
　　we will build upon her a silver
　　　　turret;
But if she is a door,
　　we will board her up with cedar
　　　　planks."
¹⁰I am a wall,
　　and my breasts are like towers.
I became in his eyes
　　as one who brings peace.

A Boast

M? ¹¹Solomon had a vineyard at
　　　　Baal-hamon;
　　he gave over the vineyard to
　　　　caretakers.
For its fruit one would have to pay
　　a thousand silver pieces.
¹²My vineyard is at my own
　　　　disposal;
　　the thousand pieces are for you,
　　　　Solomon,
　　and two hundred for the
　　　　caretakers of its fruit.

8:8-10 An answer to the brothers

The woman's brothers, who were angry with the woman in 1:6, are heard again. They think their sister is too young to be courted by a man (8:8). They will protect her virginity with barricades made of precious metal and wood (8:9). She responds to their words with the announcement that she is indeed mature and strong. Her neck and her nose have been compared to towers (4:4; 7:5); now she says that her breasts, thought to be undeveloped by her brothers, are towers. She is a source of peace (*shalom*) to the man (compared to Solomon, *shelomo*) who courts her (8:10).

Guarding a sister's virginity, and thus her value, and arranging her marriage were tasks that often fell to brothers. See, for example, Laban's interest in Rebekah (Gen 24:29-31, 50-59) and the revenge taken by Simeon and Levi for the loss of Dinah's virginity (Gen 34:25-31).

8:11-12 A boast

Vineyards have been a place where the lovers went for lovemaking (7:13); the vineyard has been a symbol for the woman (1:6; 2:15). The man has been compared to Solomon (see Introduction and 3:6-11). Now Solomon's vineyard is described as extremely valuable (7:11), but the man boasts that he has his own vineyard and, unlike Solomon, needs no caretakers. He implies that his vineyard is more valuable to him than Solomon's (7:12).

Solomon's vineyard is at Baal-hamon, which means "the master of the multitude." Is Solomon the master of the multitude? Is his vineyard the harem? Solomon had seven hundred wives and three hundred concubines (1 Kgs 11:3). If so, the man is boasting that the woman is worth more to him than Solomon's entire harem.

The Lovers' Yearnings

M ¹³You who dwell in the gardens,
    my companions are listening for
      your voice—

let me hear it!
W ¹⁴Swiftly, my lover,
    be like a gazelle or a young stag
    upon the mountains of spices.

8:13-14 The lovers' yearnings

The man has compared the woman to a garden (4:12–5:1) and she has agreed with the image (4:16; 6:2). Now he refers to the woman as one who dwells in gardens. Again he asks to hear her voice (see 2:14). She responds as she did previously, comparing him to a gazelle or young stag (see 2:9, 17) and calling him to hasten to her breasts, the mountains of spices (see 2:17; 4:6).

Ruth

Literary quality

The book of Ruth is a masterpiece of storytelling. The narrative is fictional, but the memory of David's ancestry may be historically accurate. The author's literary artistry is evident especially in the rhythmic prose and pace of the story. Care is taken with the dialogue: the older characters, Boaz and Naomi, speak in more formal and archaic language than the younger characters. Word play hints at hidden meaning, such as the echo between the words for "redeem" (*ga'al*) and "uncover" (*galah*) in the scene at the threshing floor and the double entendre of "knowing" in this emotionally charged scene (ch. 3). Other key words weave through the story: return/go back, kindness/loyalty (*hesed*), cling, empty, worthy/powerful (*hayil*), wings.

The characters are complex and well drawn. The reader is left to wonder whether Naomi did not want companions or why Boaz did not help the women sooner, why Ruth turned her attention to the older Boaz or what either woman thought would happen at the threshing floor. The plot is carefully structured. The two central chapters have similar patterns, with conversation between Ruth and Naomi surrounding the encounters between Ruth and Boaz. The first and last chapters mirror each other with discussions of kinship and the appearance of the women of Bethlehem. The story, however, does not go in a circle but moves resolutely from emptiness to fullness, desolation to redemption.

Context

The setting of the story is the time of the judges (1250–1050 B.C.) when the tribes were semi-autonomous. There was no ruler over all the twelve tribes, no capital city or central shrine. Stories in the book of Judges show it to be a rough period, a time of conflict between tribes and with neighboring peoples. A particularly horrific story is set in Bethlehem (Judg 19). Moab is the "off-stage" scene. Moab, east of Judah, on the other side of the Dead Sea, is often regarded negatively in the Bible. Its origin is traced to the incest between Lot and his elder daughter (Gen 19:37). The Moabites are remembered for their refusal to give supplies to the Israelites when they came out of the desert on their way to the Promised Land (see Judg 11:17-18). Balak, king of Moab, summoned the prophet Balaam to curse Israel (Num 22:4-6). Because of these things, there is a prohibition against admitting Moabites into the community up to the tenth generation (Deut 23:4-7; see Neh 13:1-2). In the desert Moabite women lured the people into idolatry (Num 25:1-5). In the time of the judges the Moabite king, Eglon, oppressed Israel for eighteen years (Judg 3:12-14). Later, however, David took his parents to stay in Moab for protection while he was fleeing from Saul (1 Sam 22:3-4) suggesting that he may indeed have had Moabite ancestors.

Date

The book of Ruth is virtually impossible to date. The story probably circulated orally before it was written down. The style and content suggest the time of the monarchy, perhaps the ninth–eighth century.

Theology

The most important theological question for the reader of Ruth is "where is God?" God acts only once, causing Ruth to conceive (4:13). It is reported that God has given the people food (1:6). All other mention of God is in blessings, prayers, or laments (e.g., 1:8-9, 13, 20-21). Throughout the book, however, the characters expect God to act. Most striking is the fact that the characters themselves fulfill these expectations (compare 2:12 with 3:9; 1:21 with 3:17). Is the storyteller saying that God works through the courageous actions of faithful people?

Ruth

1 **Naomi in Moab.** ¹Once back in the time of the judges there was a famine in the land; so a man from Bethlehem of Judah left home with his wife and two sons to reside on the plateau of Moab. ²The man was named Elimelech, his wife Naomi, and his sons Mahlon and Chilion; they were Ephrathites from Bethlehem of Judah. Some time after their arrival on the plateau of Moab, ³Elimelech, the husband of Naomi, died, and she was left with her two sons. ⁴They married Moabite women, one named Orpah, the other Ruth. When they had lived there about ten years, ⁵both Mahlon and Chilion died also, and the woman was left with neither her two boys nor her husband.

⁶She and her daughters-in-law then prepared to go back from the plateau of Moab because word had reached her there that the LORD had seen to his people's needs and given them food. ⁷She and her two daughters-in-law left the place where they had been living. On the road back to the land of Judah, ⁸Naomi said to her daughters-in-law, "Go back, each of you to your mother's house. May the LORD show you the same kindness as you have shown to the deceased

NAOMI IN MOAB

Ruth 1:1-18

The story is situated between the time of the judges and the beginning of the monarchy. The refrain at the end of the book of Judges—"there was no king in Israel; everyone did what was right in their own sight"—suggests a longing for a more stable situation (Judg 17:6; 21:25; see 18:1; 19:1). The book of Ruth ends with the name of Israel's best beloved king: David.

The need to relocate because of famine is mentioned more often with the patriarchs than in the period of judges (see Gen 12:10; 26:1; 42:5). It is ironic that a man from Bethlehem, which in Hebrew means "house of bread," should have to leave home with his family and go to Moab (see Introduction) because there is no bread (1:1). The occasion sets up a theme in the book of "empty" and "full" (see 1:21; 3:17). At the beginning of the story the family leaves empty of bread but full of sons.

and to me. ⁹May the LORD guide each of you to find a husband and a home in which you will be at rest." She kissed them good-bye, but they wept aloud, ¹⁰crying, "No! We will go back with you, to your people." ¹¹Naomi replied, "Go back, my daughters. Why come with me? Have I other sons in my womb who could become your husbands?ʼ ¹²Go, my daughters, for I am too old to marry again. Even if I had any such hope, or if tonight I had a husband and were to bear sons, ¹³would you wait for them and deprive yourselves of husbands until those sons grew up? No, my daughters, my lot is too bitter for you, because the LORD has extended his hand against me." ¹⁴Again they wept aloud; then Orpah kissed her mother-in-law good-bye, but Ruth clung to her.

¹⁵"See now," she said, "your sister-in-law has gone back to her people and her god. Go back after your sister-in-law!" ¹⁶But Ruth said, "Do not press me to go back and abandon you!

> Wherever you go I will go,
>   wherever you lodge I will lodge.
> Your people shall be my people
>   and your God, my God.
> ¹⁷Where you die I will die,
>   and there be buried.

May the LORD do thus to me, and more, if even death separates me from you!"

The questions "when" and "where" are answered. Now "who" is involved in this story? In the first five verses six characters are introduced and three—all the men—die. The action of the story begins with their three widows: a Judahite woman and her two Moabite daughters-in-law.

Immediately the three women set out on the road back to Judah (1:6). The repetition of two Hebrew words for "go" (ten times) and "return" (twelve times) sets the tone of this chapter. Naomi returns because her family is dead and she has heard that the famine is over. Why do the two younger women set out? Do they plan to accompany her a short distance on the road, or is their original plan to go the whole way? Three conversations turn on this question.

In the first conversation (1:8-10) Naomi indicates to her daughters-in-law that they have come far enough and prepares to say goodbye. She blesses them for their kindness (Hebrew *hesed*), the faithful love that characterizes the covenant bond, and she prays that God will grant them security. Two "houses" frame her words. She sends them back to their "mother's house." This phrase is much less frequent than "father's house." It occurs only in the betrothal scene of Rebekah (Gen 24:28) and the Song of Songs (3:4; 8:2). The phrase is probably equivalent to the "father's house." It may be used here because the conversation is between women; the mother-in-law urges them to return to their mother's house. It seems also to be used in the context of marriage. Naomi prays that each will soon be in her "husband's house."

¹⁸Naomi then ceased to urge her, for she saw she was determined to go with her.

The Return to Bethlehem. ¹⁹So they went on together until they reached Bethlehem. On their arrival there, the whole town was excited about them, and the women asked: "Can this be Naomi?" ²⁰But she said to them, "Do not call me Naomi ['Sweet']. Call me Mara ['Bitter'], for the Almighty has made my life very

---

Naomi becomes more insistent in the second conversation (1:11-14). The young women have no hope with her; she cannot give them husbands. She herself is without hope. There is a suggestion here of the practice of levirate marriage, where a man's brother marries his widow in order to raise up children for him (see Deut 25:5-10). Naomi says this is impossible; Mahlon and Chilion left no surviving brothers. Then she turns to the question of security again. The only security for women she can imagine—and the reality of the cultural situation is on her side—is in marriage. Orpah obeys her mother-in-law and sensibly turns back. But Ruth "clung," a word suggestive both of marriage and of covenant. In Genesis 2 a man leaves father and mother and clings to his wife (Gen 2:24); Ruth will not leave her mother-in-law but clings to her. In Deuteronomy the covenant people are urged to cling to God (Deut 4:4; 10:20; 11:22; 13:5).

Covenant language appears in the third conversation (1:15-18). Naomi now insists that Ruth identify with her sister-in-law and thus with the Moabite people and their god. Ruth insists on bonding with her mother-in-law and, in the best-known passage of the book, makes a lifetime commitment to Naomi, her people, and her God (see Exod 6:7; Lev 26:12). She seals the commitment with an oath in the name of YHWH, Israel's God. Naomi says no more.

THE RETURN TO BETHLEHEM

Ruth 1:19-22

Did Ruth and Naomi travel in silence the rest of the way to Bethlehem? What does Naomi's silence mean? When the two arrive, her bitterness overflows. The women of the town (who will reappear in ch. 4) seem both excited and shocked to see this woman who left more than ten years ago with a husband and two sons (1:19). Now she reappears with only a woman companion. She responds to their question by changing her name from Sweet to Bitter (1:20). There is no attempt to introduce Ruth, who will be forever known as "the Moabite woman."

Naomi blames God for her troubles (1:21). She accuses God of trying her in court and condemning her to a harsh sentence. She claims that God

bitter. [21]I went away full, but the LORD has brought me back empty. Why should you call me 'Sweet,' since the LORD has brought me to trial, and the Almighty has pronounced evil sentence on me." [22]Thus it was that Naomi came back with her Moabite daughter-in-law Ruth, who accompanied her back from the plateau of Moab. They arrived in Bethlehem at the beginning of the barley harvest.

2 **The Meeting.** [1]Naomi had a powerful relative named Boaz, through the clan of her husband Elimelech. [2]Ruth the Moabite said to Naomi, "I would like to go and glean grain in the field of anyone who will allow me." Naomi said to her, "Go ahead, my daughter." [3]So she went. The field she entered to glean after the harvesters happened to be the section belonging to Boaz, of the clan of Elimelech.

---

has made her life bitter, bringing her back to Bethlehem empty. She cries out in the tradition of the lament psalms (see especially Ps 88) and the book of Job. The lament psalms almost always turn to hope in the end. Naomi's bitter cry is the first move toward that hope.

God appears several times in this first chapter and with several names. As "LORD" (Hebrew *yhwh*) God is the one who relieved the famished people's need (1:6). Naomi prays that the Lord will take care of her daughters-in-law (1:8-9). But it is also the Lord who caused Naomi's distress (1:13) and brought her back empty (1:21). In her final outburst (1:20-21) Naomi names God "Almighty" (Hebrew *shaddai*), an ancient name going back to the time of Abraham (see Gen 17:1).

The chapter closes with a note of hope: Bethlehem, house of bread, is about to begin the barley harvest. Thus it is Passover time.

THE MEETING

Ruth 2:1-23

2:1-2 Ruth at home with Naomi

This chapter can be divided into three scenes: Ruth at home with Naomi (2:1-2); Ruth in the field of Boaz (2:3-17); Ruth at home with Naomi (2:18-23). The first scene is very brief but provides two hints that better times are ahead. The narrator introduces a rich and powerful relative of Naomi's husband. Will he come forward to help the two women? Why has he not done so already? Ruth ventures out to seek food for herself and Naomi. She has a triple right to glean, according to the law (Deut 24:19): she is a widow, "fatherless" (having left her parents), and a stranger. But will she, "the Moabite," be allowed to do so? Will this action cheer up her mother-in law?

Ruth's intention to glean reveals an important theme in this book: the presence of the needy poor. Naomi and her family went to Moab "empty"

⁴Soon, along came Boaz from Bethlehem and said to the harvesters, "The LORD be with you," and they replied, "The LORD bless you." ⁵Boaz asked the young man overseeing his harvesters, "Whose young woman is this?" ⁶The young man overseeing the harvesters answered, "She is the young Moabite who came back with Naomi from the plateau of Moab. ⁷She said, 'I would like to gather the gleanings into sheaves after the harvesters.' Ever since she came this morning she has remained here until now, with scarcely a moment's rest."

⁸Boaz then spoke to Ruth, "Listen, my daughter. Do not go to glean in anyone else's field; you are not to leave here. Stay here with my young women. ⁹Watch to see which field is to be harvested, and follow them. Have I not commanded the young men to do you no harm? When you are thirsty, go and drink from the vessels the young people have filled." ¹⁰Casting herself prostrate upon the ground, she said to him, "Why should I, a foreigner, be favored with your attention?" ¹¹Boaz answered her: "I have had a complete account of what you have done for your mother-in-law after your husband's death; you have left your father and your mother and the land of your birth, and have come to a people whom previously you did not know. ¹²May the LORD reward what you have done! May you receive a full reward from the LORD, the God of Israel, under whose wings you have come for refuge." ¹³She said, "May I prove worthy of your favor, my lord. You have comforted me. You have spoken to the heart of your servant—and I am not even one of your servants!" ¹⁴At mealtime Boaz said to her, "Come here and have something to eat; dip your bread in the sauce." Then as she sat near the harvesters, he

---

because of famine; now she and Ruth are hungry, even though God has provided food for the people in this "house of bread" (2:6). The vulnerable remain dependent on the generosity of others.

2:3-17 Ruth in the field of Boaz

The narrator cannot wait to announce more good news: The field Ruth chooses belongs to Boaz and soon the man himself appears (2:3-4). Boaz speaks first to the laborers hired to harvest his crop, greeting them with a common blessing. Then he asks the overseer about Ruth (2:5). Apparently he has spotted her among the gleaners, those following the harvesters. He asks not her name but her identity: Whose is she? Whose daughter or wife? The overseer recites the essentials—still omitting her name: She is not the daughter of anyone you know but is a foreigner, a Moabite; she does not have a husband but came with Naomi (2:6). This information, along with the observation mentioned twice that she is young, reveals Ruth to be very vulnerable. She has no protector, and Moabites are associated with illicit sexuality (see Introduction). The overseer also mentions her request to glean and her perseverance.

handed her some roasted grain and she ate her fill and had some left over. [15]As she rose to glean, Boaz instructed his young people: "Let her glean among the sheaves themselves without scolding her, [16]and even drop some handfuls and leave them for her to glean; do not rebuke her."

[17]She gleaned in the field until evening, and when she beat out what she had gleaned it came to about an ephah of barley, [18]which she took into the town and showed to her mother-in-law. Next she brought out what she had left over from the meal and gave it to her. [19]So her mother-in-law said to her, "Where did you glean today? Where did you go to work? May the one who took notice of you be blessed!" Then she told her mother-in-law with whom she had worked. "The man at whose place I

Next Boaz speaks to Ruth with a series of staccato commands: "Listen," "Do not go," "Stay," "Watch," and "drink" (2:8-9). He is the owner and in charge of gleaners as well as harvesters. His speech (like Naomi's) is formal and somewhat archaic, possibly indicating that he belongs to the older generation in contrast to all the young people around him: Ruth, whom he calls "daughter" (2:8; see 2:5, 6), the overseer (2:5, 6), and the young men (2:9, 15, 21) and young women (2:8, 22, 23) harvesters. His instructions indicate three things: his desire to have Ruth remain in his field, his awareness of her vulnerability, and his attentive care of her (permission to drink from the harvesters' water supply). In the conversation that follows she acknowledges her vulnerability and his attentive care. She had set out to glean in the field of someone in whose eyes she might find favor; now she is amazed that she has found favor (2:2, 10, 13).

Boaz, it turns out, knows who Ruth is, having heard the Bethlehem gossip (2:11-12). He prays that the Lord will reward her. The idea of taking shelter under God's wings, found in the Psalms (Pss 36:8; 61:5; 91:4), suggests the image of a mother bird protecting her young (see Exod 19:4; Deut 32:11) and also the wings of the cherubim on either side of the ark in the temple (see 1 Kgs 8:6; Isa 6:2). Ruth takes what Boaz says and turns it back toward him: *He* is the "lord" in whose eyes she hopes to find favor (2:13). In the next chapter she will ask *him* to spread his wing over her (3:9).

Boaz continues his kindness, inviting her to eat with the harvesters and making sure she has more than enough food. He also makes sure she has more than enough to glean (2:14-16). At the end of the day she has about an ephah of barley, somewhere around thirty pounds (2:17)! It has been a very good day!

2:18-23 Ruth at home with Naomi

When Ruth produces the abundance of grain plus the leftovers from lunch, Naomi is amazed. After two "where" questions, she pronounces a

"Ruth said, 'I would like to gather the gleanings into sheaves after the harvesters'" (Ruth 2:7).

worked today is named Boaz," she said. ²⁰"May he be blessed by the LORD, who never fails to show kindness to the living and to the dead," Naomi exclaimed to her daughter-in-law. She continued, "This man is a near relative of ours, one of our redeemers." ²¹"He even told me," added Ruth the Moabite, "Stay with my young people until they complete my entire harvest." ²²"You would do well, my daughter," Naomi rejoined, "to work with his young women; in someone else's field you might be insulted." ²³So she stayed gleaning with Boaz's young women until the end of the barley and wheat harvests.

3 **Ruth Again Presents Herself.** When Ruth was back with her mother-in-law, ¹Naomi said to her, "My daughter, should I not be seeking a pleasing home

---

blessing on the man who has helped her. Naomi does not yet know who this is, but she is sure some man must have made all this possible. The reader has been waiting since verse 1 for this revelation, but Ruth keeps Naomi in suspense until the end of the sentence (2:19). As soon as Naomi hears the name Boaz, she tells Ruth that he is someone on whom they can count for help. He is a *go'el*, a "redeemer" (2:20). The *go'el* had responsibilities to help a debtor regain land (Lev 25:25) or be released from slavery (Lev 25:48); he also had responsibility to avenge one's murder (Num 35:19, 21). The responsibility of a man to marry his deceased brother's widow is nowhere included among the responsibilities of a *go'el*, and Naomi herself seems to think that this duty of levirate marriage applies only to a brother (1:11), not to a larger kinship. So what does she expect of Boaz, a member of Elimilech's clan? Naomi's words are also ambiguous: who is it "who never fails to show kindness to the living and to the dead"? The Hebrew allows for either subject: the Lord or Boaz ("he").

Naomi has been transformed by this good news. She is now speaking to Ruth in full sentences. She is blessing the Lord whom she earlier accused. She now thinks of Ruth as part of the family: "near relative of *ours*, one of *our* redeemers" (emphasis added).

In the final interchange between the two women there is an amusing confusion of words (2:21-22). Ruth reports (incorrectly) that Boaz has told her to stay with his "young men"; Naomi, well aware of her daughter-in-law's vulnerability, points out that it would be better to work with his "young women." The word translated "stay" is the same verb translated as "cling" in 1:14, emphasizing the inadvisability of "clinging" to the young men. Ruth obeys Naomi, staying with the young women throughout the grain harvest. The time between the beginning of the barley harvest and the end of the wheat harvest is usually calculated as seven weeks, the time between Passover and Pentecost (see Deut 16:9-10).

for you? ²Now! Is not Boaz, whose young women you were working with, a relative of ours? This very night he will be winnowing barley at the threshing floor. ³Now, go bathe and anoint yourself; then put on your best attire and go down to the threshing floor. Do not make yourself known to the man before he has finished eating and drinking. ⁴But when he lies down, take note of the place where he lies; then go uncover a place at his feet and you lie down. He will then tell you what to do." ⁵"I will do whatever you say," Ruth replied. ⁶She went down to the threshing floor and did just as her mother-in-law had instructed her.

⁷Boaz ate and drank to his heart's content, and went to lie down at the edge of the pile of grain. She crept up, uncovered a place at his feet, and lay down. ⁸Midway through the night, the

RUTH AGAIN PRESENTS HERSELF

Ruth 3:1-18

3:1-6 Ruth at home with Naomi

Chapter 3 can also be divided into three scenes: Ruth at home with Naomi (3:1-6); Ruth at the threshing floor with Boaz (3:7-15); Ruth at home with Naomi (3:16-18). In chapter 2 Boaz addressed Ruth with a series of commands (2:8-9); in the first scene of chapter 3 a revived Naomi gives the commands. Naomi had prayed that her two daughters-in-law would find rest in the home of a husband (1:9). Now she sets out to find that "rest" for Ruth (3:1). Ruth is to beautify herself and find Boaz at the threshing floor (3:3). This instruction already seems scandalous; should a young woman go alone at night to a place where men have been working all day and drinking through the evening? Naomi's second instruction is even more shocking: uncover the sleeping Boaz and lie down next to him (3:4)! Ruth is to uncover his "feet." But this is not the common word for "feet"; it may also connote "legs." In addition, "feet" is the common euphemism for genitals. So it is unclear how much of Boaz Ruth is supposed to uncover, but Naomi's words are certainly suggestive. Ruth's response is simple assent (3:5). Her words echo Israel's response to God in the covenant making at Sinai: "Everything the LORD has said, we will do" (Exod 19:8).

A question arises concerning why Boaz is winnowing barley at the end of the wheat harvest. Were the sheaves stored and all the grain winnowed at once?

3:7-15 Ruth at the threshing floor with Boaz

This section is characterized by the absence of proper names; each character is only named once (3:7, 9). It is night at the threshing floor and

man gave a start and groped about, only to find a woman lying at his feet. ⁹"Who are you?" he asked. She replied, "I am your servant Ruth. Spread the wing of your cloak over your servant, for you are a redeemer." ¹⁰He said, "May the LORD bless you, my daughter! You have been even more loyal now than before in not going after the young men, whether poor or rich. ¹¹Now rest assured, my daughter, I will do for you whatever you say; all my townspeople know you to be a worthy woman. ¹²Now, I am in fact a redeemer, but there is another redeemer closer than I. ¹³Stay where you are for tonight, and tomorrow, if he will act as redeemer for you, good. But if he will not, as the LORD lives, I will do it myself. Lie there until morning." ¹⁴So she lay at his feet until morning, but rose before anyone could recognize another, for Boaz had said, "Let it not be known that this woman came to the threshing floor." ¹⁵Then he said to her, "Take off the shawl you are wearing; hold it firmly." When she did so, he poured out six measures of barley and helped her lift the bundle; then he himself left for the town.

whatever happens is shrouded in secrecy. Ruth has indeed followed Naomi's instructions. Boaz is startled awake in the middle of the night—because he is cold? Or aware of another presence? The narrator takes the viewpoint of Boaz: He groped around and look! a woman at his feet (3:8)! He demands: Who are you! Her response recalls their conversation in the field, but there are significant differences. Earlier she said she was not his servant (2:13); now she identifies herself as "servant" (3:9). But she has changed the term for "servant" from *shiphhah* to *amah*; the *amah* was eligible for marriage with her master whereas the *shiphhah* was not. Boaz had described her taking shelter under the Lord's wing; she asks Boaz to spread the wing of his cloak over her. In this context the request suggests sexual relations and is tantamount to a proposal of marriage (see Deut 23:1; Ezek 16:8). She continues: You are a redeemer, a *go'el*. What does Ruth expect? Nowhere else does the responsibility of the *go'el* include marriage to a relative's widow. Does Ruth, a Moabite, not know that? Is she only picking up the word from Naomi, understanding it (correctly) to be someone who is responsible to help family members in need? Is Ruth being creative? Is this part of the law that we simply do not know? (Notice also that it is Ruth who is telling Boaz what to do, not the reverse as Naomi suggested.)

Boaz describes Ruth's second act of loyalty (*hesed*) as greater than the first (3:10). Is the first act her commitment to Naomi, which Boaz mentioned earlier (see 1:8; 2:11)? Is her offer of marriage to Boaz a further commitment to Naomi? Ruth was not bound by the laws of levirate marriage. She has no brothers-in-law and she is a foreigner. She could have married any of the young men. But such a marriage might have separated her from Naomi, whereas marriage to a relative will not.

¹⁶She, meanwhile, went home to her mother-in-law, who asked, "How did things go, my daughter?" So she told her all the man had done for her, ¹⁷and concluded, "He gave me these six measures of barley and said, 'Do not go back to your mother-in-law empty.'" ¹⁸Naomi then said, "Wait here, my daughter, until you learn what happens, for the man will not rest, but will settle the matter today."

4 Boaz Marries Ruth. ¹Boaz went to the gate and took a seat there. Along came the other redeemer of whom he had spoken. Boaz called to him by name, "Come, sit here." And he did so. ²Then Boaz picked out ten of the elders of the town and asked them to sit nearby. When they had done this, ³he said to the other redeemer: "Naomi, who has come back from the plateau of Moab, is putting up for sale the piece of land that

---

Now Boaz echoes Ruth's words: whatever you say (3:11). He identifies her as "a worthy woman" (Hebrew, *eshet hayil*). He was introduced with the same adjective, "powerful, worthy" (2:1, *ish gibbor hayil*). He has erased the social distinction between them; she is no longer to be identified as "servant." In some versions of the Jewish Bible the book of Ruth comes immediately after the book of Proverbs. The final poem in that book begins with the question: "Who can find a woman of worth?" (*eshet hayil*; Prov 31:10). Boaz says, "I have."

Boaz accepts Ruth's identification of him as a "redeemer" and uses the root word "redeem" six times in verses 12-13. But there is a further twist in the plot, a closer relative. So secrecy must be maintained. Ruth leaves at the first light of dawn (3:14-15).

3:16-18 Ruth at home with Naomi

This is the last conversation between the two women; neither will speak again. Ruth reports on the night's happenings and gives her mother-in-law the gift of grain. Boaz admires Ruth's care for Naomi; he too cares for her. He has again acted in the Lord's name, not sending Ruth back to Naomi "empty" (3:17; see Naomi's complaint against the Lord in 1:21). Naomi assures Ruth (and the reader) that the complication will be solved "today" (3:18).

BOAZ MARRIES RUTH

Ruth 4:1-22

In this chapter the scene returns to the public view: Boaz and the "other redeemer" at the town gate (4:1-12); the women's celebration over the birth of a son (4:14-17); a closing genealogy (4:18-22). Only in verse 13, which

belonged to our kinsman Elimelech. ⁴So I thought I would inform you. Before those here present, including the elders of my people, purchase the field; act as redeemer. But if you do not want to do it, tell me so, that I may know, for no one has a right of redemption prior to yours, and mine is next." He answered, "I will act as redeemer."

⁵Boaz continued, "When you acquire the field from Naomi, you also acquire responsibility for Ruth the Moabite, the widow of the late heir, to raise up a family for the deceased on his estate." ⁶The re-

deemer replied, "I cannot exercise my right of redemption for that would endanger my own estate. You do it in my place, for I cannot." ⁷Now it used to be the custom in Israel that, to make binding a contract of redemption or exchange, one party would take off a sandal and give it to the other. This was the form of attestation in Israel. ⁸So the other redeemer, in saying to Boaz, "Acquire it for yourself," drew off his sandal. ⁹Boaz then said to the elders and to all the people, "You are witnesses today that I have acquired from Naomi all the holdings of Elimelech, Chil-

reports in short order the marriage of Boaz and Ruth and the birth of their son, is there the suggestion of a private space.

4:1-12 At the town gate

The town gate is the setting for the exercise of law, business, and political judgment. Every man could be expected to pass through the gate to the fields and back every day. Boaz summons the "other redeemer" and ten elders who will function as witnesses to settle the matter (the reader thinks) of his marriage to Ruth (4:1-2). He calls the "other redeemer" *peloni almoni*, a Hebrew way of saying "Mr. So-and-So." Why does he do this? Surely he knows the man's name! There is no need to protect him since there is no negative judgment against him. The narrative effect of his "non-name" is to diminish this character even more than Orpah in chapter 1; he is simply not worth naming!

The reader is surprised that Boaz begins not with the issue of marriage but with the sale of a piece of land (4:3-4). Why did we not know Naomi had land? Why does she seem so destitute? What has happened to the land since Elimilech and his family left Bethlehem? How does Boaz have authority to dispose of the land? The narrator does not answer these questions. The issue of land, however, is appropriate to the responsibility of the *go'el*. (The root word "redeem" occurs four times in verse 4.) A reasonable scenario is this: When Elimilech left Bethlehem, someone else began to farm the abandoned land. Naomi's return coincided with the harvest, and no claim to the land could be made until the harvest was complete. In reclaiming the land Naomi seems to have two choices: find someone to cultivate it or sell it. If she puts it up for sale, the *go'el* has the responsibility to acquire

ion and Mahlon. [10]I also acquire Ruth the Moabite, the widow of Mahlon, as my wife, in order to raise up a family for her late husband on his estate, so that the name of the deceased may not perish from his people and his place. Do you witness this today?" [11]All those at the gate, including the elders, said, "We do. May the LORD make this woman come into your house like Rachel and Leah, who between them built up the house of Israel. Prosper in Ephrathah! Bestow a name in Bethlehem! [12]With the offspring the LORD will give you from this young woman, may your house become like the house of Perez, whom Tamar bore to Judah."

---

it (Lev 25:25) so that the land will remain within the clan (see Lev 25:10; Num 36:8). Even if she sells it, the land is to be returned at the next jubilee year (see Lev 25:28). Thus Boaz seems to be acting out of courtesy to the man who has the first right of refusal. The man no doubt recognizes that he will have to return the land and that he is also taking responsibility for Naomi's welfare by purchasing it. He agrees to act as *go'el*.

Then Boaz reveals the surprise: Ruth is part of the package (4:5)! This is not only to be an act of "redemption" but also a levirate marriage. The Hebrew is confusing here. What is written is "*I* will acquire Ruth," but the transmitters of the text in early medieval period revocalized it to say, "*you* must acquire Ruth." (The NABRE translation clarifies that "responsibility for Ruth" is the object of acquisition.) Although the two options change the plot considerably, the consequence is similar: economic loss. If Boaz marries Ruth, there will probably be an heir to whom the land will revert in the name of Ruth's first husband. If the "other redeemer" marries her, he will have to support her, plus any children she may have. In the situation of levirate marriage no attention is given to the *levir's* current marital situation. "Mr. So-and-So" probably already has a wife and children. In addition, Ruth is a Moabite, which may cause the man to hesitate. It is too much. He relinquishes his right and responsibility (4:6). The ritual of relinquishing is otherwise unknown. The "other redeemer" takes off his sandal and gives it to Boaz as a sign that Boaz now has the right and responsibility to act (4:7-8). There are echoes of the ritual when a widow is rejected by her brother-in-law: she is to take off his sandal and spit in his face (Deut 25:8-10). In that ritual the potential husband is shamed; here there is no shaming.

Boaz calls on the witnesses to confirm the transaction: he acquires the land and Ruth; he acts as *go'el* and *levir* (4:9-10). All the people at the gate—the ten elders and the crowd that has gathered—bless Boaz and his marriage (4:11-12). (Note: they ignore the land.) They pray for the prosperity of Boaz and that the marriage be blessed with children—thus he will be able to

¹³Boaz took Ruth. When they came together as husband and wife, the LORD enabled her to conceive and she bore a son. ¹⁴Then the women said to Naomi, "Blessed is the LORD who has not failed to provide you today with a redeemer. May he become famous in Israel! ¹⁵He will restore your life and be the support of your old age, for his mother is the daughter-in-law who loves you. She is worth more to you than seven sons!" ¹⁶Naomi took the boy, cradled him against her breast, and cared for him. ¹⁷The neighbor women joined the cele-

---

"Bestow a name." They pray that Ruth may be like the matriarchs of Israel: Rachel, the beloved wife; Leah, mother of six of the twelve tribes (plus two from her maidservant, Zilpah); and Tamar, ancestor of Boaz. Each of these women endured unusual marriage circumstances. Leah was substituted for Rachel on Jacob's wedding night and Rachel wedded only later (Gen 29:21-30). Like Ruth, Tamar was a foreign woman caught in a troublesome situation of levirate marriage (see Gen 38). After the death of two husbands, she disguised herself and tricked her father-in-law Judah into fathering her twin sons. Judah judged her "more righteous" than himself. Each of these women was *eshet hayil*, a woman of worth.

The Lord has been mentioned in blessings throughout the book, but only twice does the Lord act: giving food to end the famine (1:6) and now giving Ruth and Boaz a son (4:13). Although the plot demands it, this conception is not at all certain. Ruth was married to her first husband for ten years without bearing a child; Boaz is no longer young. The child is a gift of God.

4:14-17 The women's celebration

The women of Bethlehem, who listened to Naomi's challenge to God in 1:21, now bless God for providing for her. She has been given a redeemer, a *go'el*. This is the new heir who will care for her old age, not Boaz, although he too is now her *go'el*. The catalyst for God's action is Ruth, mother of the child, wife of Boaz. The word "love" appears only here in this book; redemption has come through Ruth's love of Naomi. Ruth, to whom Naomi hardly spoke in her bitterness, is worth more than this new baby, worth more than even seven sons! Seven is the number for fullness. The new baby boy helps heal Naomi's heart from the loss of her two boys in Moab. The neighbor women name the baby, a unique occurrence in the Old Testament (4:17). Usually either the mother or father gives the name. In the New Testament, however, the neighbors attempt to name Elizabeth's baby Zechariah for his father (see Luke 1:58-59).

bration: "A son has been born to Naomi!" They named him Obed. He was the father of Jesse, the father of David.

[18]These are the descendants of Perez: Perez was the father of Hezron, [19]Hezron was the father of Ram, Ram was the father of Amminadab, [20]Amminadab was the father of Nahshon, Nahshon was the father of Salma, [21]Salma was the father of Boaz, Boaz was the father of Obed, [22]Obed was the father of Jesse, and Jesse became the father of David.

4:18-22 A genealogy

The book closes with a genealogy, possibly a later addition. The genealogy begins with Perez, son of Tamar, and ends with David, Israel's best-loved king. At the significant seventh and tenth positions in the list are found Boaz and David. The story has moved the reader from the time of the judges to the time of the monarchy; the genealogy reaches farther back to the time of the patriarchs. It is ironic that no women are mentioned in the genealogy that closes this story of two valiant women. The only genealogy in which Ruth will appear is the genealogy of Jesus (Matt 1:5).

Lamentations

Name and authorship

In the Hebrew Bible this book is called *Eykah* from the first word of chapters 1, 2, and 4. *Eykah*, an exclamation of astonishment ("how!"), captures the tone. In the Talmud and other early Jewish works it is called *Qinot*, "Lamentations." This title is reflected also in the Greek and Latin translations. Greek and Latin manuscripts also identify Jeremiah as the author, although this late attribution is more symbolic than factual. Jeremiah, who weeps over the impending destruction and exile (Jer 8:23; 9:9, 16, 19), is the "patron saint" of lamenters.

Date and historical background

Both the content and the traditional identification with Jeremiah have associated this book with the destruction of Jerusalem by the Babylonians in 587 B.C. The Septuagint introduces the book thus: "After Israel was taken captive and Jerusalem made desolate, Jeremiah sat weeping and lamenting this lamentation over Jerusalem." Following this tradition, the writing would have been sometime in the sixth century. The style of language is similar to other writers of this period, such as Jeremiah and Ezekiel. There are no specific indications in the content, however, that suggest which tragedy is being lamented. Thus these poems have been applied to many disasters throughout the millennia.

Liturgical use

In the Jewish tradition the book of Lamentations is read on the ninth of Ab to commemorate several tragedies. Solomon's temple fell to the Babylonians sometime between the seventh and tenth of Ab (see 2 Kgs 25:8-9; Jer 52:12), and the second temple fell to the Romans on the ninth of Ab in A.D. 70. In Christian tradition Lamentations is often used during the Triduum (Holy Thursday to Holy Saturday).

Literary artistry

The five poems in this collection represent both the dirge (chs. 1, 2, 4) and the lament (chs. 3, 5). The dirge, a funeral song, often reports the cry of the mourners, the proclamation of death, and the reaction of the bystand-ers. The individual lament (ch. 3) usually begins with a cry to God, contin-ues with some of these elements—a description of distress, a plea for help, a demand for vengeance, an attempt to persuade God—and ends with a turn to hope (see, for example, Pss 3; 5; 6). The communal lament contains some of the same elements but is the community's response to a national disaster (see, for example, Pss 74; 79).

Each of these poems is based on the alphabet. The first four are true acrostics. In chapters 1, 2, and 4 the first letter of each three-line verse spells out the Hebrew alphabet in order. The sixty-six verses of chapter 3 represent a more developed acrostic, with three verses for the first letter, three for the second, etc. Chapter 5 has twenty-two verses, suggesting the twenty-two letters of the alphabet, but the first letters of the verses are random. The first three chapters are longer, sixty-six lines each. Chapter 4 has forty-four lines (two lines per verse) and chapter 5 only twenty-two. The predominant rhythm of accents in each two-line unit is 3 accents + 2 accents. This "limp-ing" rhythm is called *qinah* ("lament") because of its association with mourning, although it is found in other contexts also. It is suggested that the three long chapters of the book followed by the two short chapters is also in imitation of the *qinah* rhythm.

The city is personified as "Daughter," the woman violated, the mother weeping for her children. Two names are used for the city, Zion (see 1:6) and Jerusalem (see 2:13); sometimes the name of the region, Judah, appears (see 1:15). The identification of a city as female is common in the ancient Near East. Four voices are heard in the poems: a narrator, Daughter Zion, a heroic man, and the community. Three of the voices interweave through-out the poems. The heroic man appears only in chapter 3. The voice that is never heard is that of God.

City = daughter

Name of region = Judah

Lamentations

The Desolation of Jerusalem

1 ¹How solitary sits the city,
  once filled with people.
She who was great among the
    nations
  is now like a widow.
Once a princess among the
    provinces,
  now a toiling slave.
²She weeps incessantly in the night,
  her cheeks damp with tears.
She has no one to comfort her
  from all her lovers;
Her friends have all betrayed her,
  and become her enemies.

³Judah has gone into exile,
  after oppression and harsh
    labor;
She dwells among the nations,
  yet finds no rest:

All her pursuers overtake her
  in the narrow straits.

⁴The roads to Zion mourn,
  empty of pilgrims to her feasts.
All her gateways are desolate,
  her priests groan,
Her young women grieve;
  her lot is bitter.

⁵Her foes have come out on top,
  her enemies are secure;
Because the LORD has afflicted her
  for her many rebellions.
Her children have gone away,
  captive before the foe.

⁶From daughter Zion has gone
  all her glory:
Her princes have become like rams
  that find no pasture.

THE DESOLATION OF JERUSALEM

Lamentations 1:1-22

In this twenty-two verse acrostic (see Introduction), each verse (except 1:7) consists of three two-line units (called a, b, and c throughout the commentary). The chapter falls into two equal sections: the narrator in verses 1-11 describes the desolation of Jerusalem; Jerusalem herself cries out in lament in verses 12-22.

1:1-11 Jerusalem's desolation

The chapter begins with the cry, *'eykah*, "How"! The cry echoes Isaiah's lament over once-faithful Jerusalem (Isa 1:21). The former glory of Jerusalem, described as a woman, is contrasted with her present desperate state.

They have gone off exhausted
    before their pursuers.
⁷Jerusalem remembers
    in days of wretched
        homelessness,
All the precious things she once
    had
    in days gone by.
But when her people fell into the
    hands of the foe,
    and she had no help,
Her foes looked on and laughed
    at her collapse.

⁸Jerusalem has sinned grievously,
    therefore she has become a
        mockery;
Those who honored her now
    demean her,
    for they saw her nakedness;
She herself groans out loud,
    and turns away.

⁹Her uncleanness is on her skirt;
    she has no thought of her future.
Her downfall is astonishing,
    with no one to comfort her.
"Look, O Lᴏʀᴅ, at my misery;
    how the enemy triumphs!"

¹⁰The foe stretched out his hands
    to all her precious things;
She has seen the nations
    enter her sanctuary,
Those you forbade to come
    into your assembly.

¹¹All her people groan,
    searching for bread;
They give their precious things for
    food,
    to retain the breath of life.
"Look, O Lᴏʀᴅ, and pay attention
    to how I have been demeaned!

Those she trusted have abandoned her. "Lovers" and "friends" are covenant terms for political allies. The refrain heard throughout this chapter begins here: "She has no one to comfort her" (1:2; see 1:9, 16, 17, 21).

After suffering the economic devastation of Babylonian rule and the anguish of the siege, Judah has gone into exile. The "rest" promised in the exodus and fulfilled in the land has now been lost (see Deut 12:9; Ps 95:11). The description of her defeat is enclosed by the word "pursuers" (1:3, 6). Her pursuers overtake her in the "narrow straits" (1:3; *metsarim*); the word echoes the Hebrew term for Egypt (*mitsrayim*), the place where the exodus began. Zion is empty; even the roads and gates grieve (1:4). The people— priests and princes, women and children—are driven into exile (1:6). The enemy has won. But who is the enemy? This affliction comes from God because Jerusalem has rebelled (1:5). This is the first of several admissions of guilt (see 1:8-9, 14, 18). Her glory is lost, and it is her own fault.

Verse 7 is too long for the three-line pattern. Various solutions have been proposed. Some translations omit either the b or c line; others move the b line to verse 6. Perhaps the chapter circulated in two forms, one with the second line, another with the third. The NABRE has chosen to keep all the lines in the order we now have in the Hebrew text. The verse moves to a different perspective. Verses 1-6 described defeat and departure as immediate

¹²Come, all who pass by the way,
    pay attention and see:
Is there any pain like my pain,
    which has been ruthlessly
        inflicted upon me,
With which the LORD has tor-
    mented me
    on the day of his blazing wrath?

¹³From on high he hurled fire down
    into my very bones;
He spread out a net for my feet,
    and turned me back.
He has left me desolate,
    in misery all day long.

¹⁴The yoke of my rebellions is
    bound together,
    fastened by his hand.
His yoke is upon my neck;
    he has made my strength fail.
The Lord has delivered me into the
    grip
    of those I cannot resist.

¹⁵All my valiant warriors
    my Lord has cast away;
He proclaimed a feast against me
    to crush my young men;
My Lord has trodden in the wine
    press
    virgin daughter Judah.

¹⁶For these things I weep—My eyes!
    My eyes!
They stream with tears!
How far from me is anyone to
    comfort,
    anyone to restore my life.
My children are desolate;
    the enemy has prevailed."

¹⁷Zion stretches out her hands,
    with no one to comfort her;
The LORD has ordered against Jacob
    his foes all around;
Jerusalem has become in their
    midst
    a thing unclean.

---

experiences; in verse 7 Jerusalem remembers what she has lost and what she has suffered. A variation on the refrain bemoaning the absence of a comforter appears: here she has no helper (see Pss 22:12; 72:12; 107:12; Isa 63:5).

The image of Jerusalem in verses 8-9 is that of a demeaned woman. She is shamed by nakedness; her uncleanness (menstrual blood?) is visible on her skirt. She is utterly disgraced. (Compare the prophetic description of the fall of Babylon, Isa 47:1-6.)

The next few verses are set off by an inclusion (the repetition of a word or phrase): Jerusalem herself interrupts the narration of her disaster, crying out to the Lord to look at her misery (see 9c and 11c). The inclusion surrounds further description of the siege and defeat of the city. The enemy has taken her treasures and dared to enter the temple; famine has gripped the people (1:10-11). Her "precious things" are lost: the sacred vessels of the temple taken by the enemy, the children bartered for food.

1:12-22 Jerusalem's cry

Now Daughter Zion begins her lament. The call to witness her pain leads into an accusation of the Lord for inflicting this misery on her. It happened "on the day of his blazing wrath," a day described by the prophets

¹⁸"The LORD is in the right;
 I had defied his command.
Listen, all you peoples,
 and see my pain:
My young women and young men
 have gone into captivity.

¹⁹I cried out to my lovers,
 but they failed me.
My priests and my elders
 perished in the city;
How desperately they searched for
 food,
  to save their lives!

²⁰Look, O LORD, at the anguish I
 suffer!
My stomach churns,

And my heart recoils within me:
 How bitter I am!
Outside the sword bereaves—
 indoors, there is death.

²¹Hear how I am groaning;
 there is no one to comfort me.
All my enemies hear of my misery
 and rejoice
 over what you have done.
Bring on the day you proclaimed,
 and let them become like me!

²²Let all their evil come before you
 and deal with them
As you have so ruthlessly dealt
 with me
 for all my rebellions.

(see Isa 13:9-13; Zeph 2:2-3). She is attacked from within (fire in her bones) and without (a net to trip her up) (1:13). This has happened, however, because of her own sins. God has bound them up into a yoke that presses down on her neck and forces her to the ground (1:14). The judgment against her is described as harvest, a common prophetic image (see Joel 4:13; Hos 6:11). She has been trodden like grapes in the wine press; her young men have been crushed like grain at the feast. God has tossed away her best warriors like chaff and given her into the power of her enemies (1:15).

Jerusalem cries out in agony—no comforter, no children—only tears (1:16). The narrator interrupts to describe Jerusalem's situation and the Lord's decree, summoning her enemies (1:17). Jerusalem ends this accusation against God, not with the turn to hope that is commonly found in the psalms of communal lament but with testimony that God is just in inflicting this suffering on her because of her sins (1:18a).

A new summons to "listen" begins and ends the next section (1:18b and 21a). All those who might have helped, who might have comforted, are listed: the young, political allies, religious leaders. But they are all focused on saving themselves (1:19). So Jerusalem calls again on the Lord to see how she suffers. Again the suffering is described as both within and without (compare 1:13), but now she is like a house with killing outside in the street and death inside (1:20).

The chapter concludes with a prayer for vengeance: may my enemies suffer for their guilt at your hands as I have. Bring on the day the prophets describe (1:21-22). In the final line Jerusalem collapses from her pain.

My groans are many,
my heart is sick."

The Lord's Wrath and Zion's Ruin

2 ¹How the Lord in his wrath
has abhorred daughter Zion,
Casting down from heaven to earth
the glory of Israel,
Not remembering his footstool
on the day of his wrath!

²The Lord has devoured without
pity
all of Jacob's dwellings;
In his fury he has razed
daughter Judah's defenses,
Has brought to the ground in
dishonor
a kingdom and its princes.

³In blazing wrath, he cut down
entirely
the horn of Israel;
He withdrew the support of his
right hand

when the enemy approached;
He burned against Jacob like a
blazing fire
that consumes everything in its
path.

⁴He bent his bow like an enemy;
the arrow in his right hand
Like a foe, he killed
all those held precious;
On the tent of daughter Zion
he poured out his wrath like fire.

⁵The Lord has become the enemy,
he has devoured Israel:
Devoured all its strongholds,
destroyed its defenses,
Multiplied moaning and groaning
throughout daughter Judah.

⁶He laid waste his booth like a
garden,
destroyed his shrine;
The LORD has blotted out in Zion
feast day and sabbath,

THE LORD'S WRATH AND ZION'S RUIN

Lamentations 2:1-22

Chapter 2 also has twenty-two verses of three lines each. The beginning letter of each verse spells the alphabet. In this chapter, in contrast to chapter 1, the narrator/poet speaks for the first nineteen verses; in the last three verses Zion cries out in lament. As in chapter 1, Zion is portrayed as a woman. The theme of chapter 2 is clear: The Lord has caused Zion's misery (2:1-9, 17, 20-22). Yet the Lord is Zion's only recourse; only the Lord can help her (2:18-20).

In verses 1-9 the Lord is the subject of almost every sentence; only in verse 7c do the enemies find a voice. The Lord's blazing wrath burns through the section; words for "wrath" or "fury" appear in every one of the first four verses. In verse 4 the Lord, described as a murderous warrior, acts "like an enemy." In verse 5 the poet acknowledges the truth: "The Lord has become the enemy." The Lord has rejected his chosen city and the temple, his footstool (2:1). He has "devoured" (literally, "swallowed up") all Judah's buildings and defenses (2:2, 5). He has crushed the kingdom

Has scorned in fierce wrath
    king and priest.

⁷The Lord has rejected his altar,
    spurned his sanctuary;
He has handed over to the enemy
    the walls of its strongholds.
They shout in the house of the
    LORD
    as on a feast day.

⁸The LORD was bent on destroying
    the wall of daughter Zion:
He stretched out the measuring
    line;
    did not hesitate to devour,
Brought grief on rampart and wall
    till both succumbed.

⁹Her gates sank into the ground;
    he smashed her bars to bits.
Her king and her princes are
    among the nations;
    instruction is wanting,
Even her prophets do not obtain
    any vision from the LORD.

¹⁰The elders of daughter Zion
    sit silently on the ground;

They cast dust on their heads
    and dress in sackcloth;
The young women of Jerusalem
    bow their heads to the ground.

¹¹My eyes are spent with tears,
    my stomach churns;
My bile is poured out on the
    ground
    at the brokenness of the
       daughter of my people,
As children and infants collapse
    in the streets of the town.

¹²They cry out to their mothers,
    "Where is bread and wine?"
As they faint away like the
    wounded
    in the streets of the city,
As their life is poured out
    in their mothers' arms.

¹³To what can I compare you—to
    what can I liken you—
    O daughter Jerusalem?
What example can I give in order to
    comfort you,
    virgin daughter Zion?

(2:2), cutting off its strength (the Hebrew idiom is "horn," 2:3). He has "multiplied moaning and groaning"; the Hebrew phrase has the same rhyming effect, *ta'aniyyah wa'aniyyah* (2:5).

Verse 6 returns to the painful truth (see 2:1) that the Lord has destroyed even the sacred places dedicated to his worship; "booth" and "shrine," "altar" and "sanctuary," all suggest the temple. All the liturgical worship—feast day and Sabbath—and the leadership are wiped out. The sacred space is desecrated by the riotous presence of the enemy (2:6-7). The Lord measures Zion like a builder but instead is bent on destroying walls and gates (2:8-9a).

The subject changes in verse 9b; the people respond to the disaster. What was said earlier (1:1, 7) is true: They have no help, no comforter. The leaders are "among the nations," that is, in exile. There is no instruction (Hebrew, *torah*) and the prophets receive no vision. All the people, from old men to young women, respond with traditional mourning rites: silence, sitting on

For your breach is vast as the sea;
　who could heal you?

¹⁴Your prophets provided you
　　visions
　of whitewashed illusion;
They did not lay bare your guilt,
　in order to restore your fortunes;
They saw for you only oracles
　of empty deceit.

¹⁵All who pass by on the road,
　clap their hands at you;
They hiss and wag their heads
　over daughter Jerusalem:
"Is this the city they used to call

perfect in beauty and joy of all
　the earth?"

¹⁶They open their mouths against
　you,
　all your enemies;
They hiss and gnash their teeth,
　saying, "We have devoured her!
How we have waited for this day—
　we have lived to see it!"

¹⁷The LORD has done what he
　planned.
He has fulfilled the threat
Decreed from days of old,
　destroying without pity!

---

the ground, wearing sackcloth, putting dust or ashes on their heads (see Gen 37:34; Jer 6:26; Job 2:11-13; Esth 4:1-3). But the sight of the starving children brings the poet to bitter grief (2:11). They faint like wounded warriors and die in their mother's arms (2:12).

The poet can find no metaphor to give meaning to Zion's suffering. "Vast as the sea" is another way to say "farther than anyone can imagine" (see Ps 139:9). In chapter 1, Zion acknowledged that the disaster came upon her because of her guilt (1:18). In chapter 2 a reason is given for her guilt: the prophets have prophesied false peace, so Zion did not repent (2:14; see Jer 6:13-15; 14:11-16). Now Zion has become a mockery; passersby taunt her with phrases from the psalms: "perfect in beauty, and joy of all the earth" (2:15; see Pss 48:3; 50:2). The enemies think that they have destroyed Zion by their own power: *They* have devoured; this is *their* day (2:16). But it is really the day of the *Lord's* wrath (see v. 22); it is the *Lord* who has done this (2:17). This restatement of the theme binds verses 1-17 into a unit. It also suggests the reason for Zion's hope: the Lord has struck; only the Lord can heal.

The poet exhorts Zion to cry out to the Lord (2:18-19). Throughout the Old Testament, when Israel cries out in distress, the Lord answers. When they are enslaved in Egypt and cry out, God calls Moses and begins the exodus (Exod 2:23-25). Whenever they are oppressed during the settlement period they cry out and God sends a judge to deliver them (see Judg 3:9, 15; 4:3). The encouragement of the poet is based on precedent. He encourages Zion to pray with tears night and day. It was believed in the ancient world that the heart liquefied with sorrow and that tears were the outpour-

He let the enemy gloat over you
and exalted the horn of your
foes.

[18]Cry out to the Lord from your
heart,
wall of daughter Zion!
Let your tears flow like a torrent
day and night;
Give yourself no rest,
no relief for your eyes.

[19]Rise up! Wail in the night,
at the start of every watch;
Pour out your heart like water
before the Lord;
Lift up your hands to him
for the lives of your children,
Who collapse from hunger
at the corner of every street.
[20]"Look, O LORD, and pay attention:
to whom have you been so
ruthless?

Must women eat their own
offspring,
the very children they have
borne?
Are priest and prophet to be slain
in the sanctuary of the Lord?

[21]They lie on the ground in the
streets,
young and old alike;
Both my young women and young
men
are cut down by the sword;
You killed them on the day of your
wrath,
slaughtered without pity.

[22]You summoned as to a feast day
terrors on every side;
On the day of the LORD's wrath,
none survived or escaped.
Those I have borne and nurtured,
my enemy has utterly destroyed."

---

ing of the melted heart (see Ps 22:15; Isa 13:7). Zion is to pray, not for herself but for her children. The fourth line of verse 19 breaks the pattern of three-line verses, but Zion's agony also breaks every pattern.

2:20-22 Zion's lament

The last three verses are Zion's lament. She cries out to the Lord, but her only request is that God take note of the extent of her suffering. The rest of her lament is a description of the disaster. Everything that can be counted on has been lost. Religious leaders are killed even inside the sanctuary and mothers eat their own children. Cannibalism is known to be a horrible result of desperate famine. Young and old lie in the streets. Have they collapsed from hunger? Do they lie there dead and unburied?

Zion concludes her lament with an accusation against God: "You killed them"; "You summoned . . . terrors." The day of the Lord's wrath is mentioned twice (2:21, 22). God has held a terrible festival; Zion's children have been slaughtered as the sacrifice (see Isa 34:1-8; Zeph 1:7-9). The "terrors on every side," announced by Jeremiah, have arrived (see Jer 6:25; 20:3-5). Zion mourns the children destroyed by her enemy; the enemy is God.

The Voice of a Suffering Individual

3 ¹I am one who has known affliction
under the rod of God's anger,
²One whom he has driven and
forced to walk
in darkness, not in light;
³Against me alone he turns his
hand—
again and again all day long.

⁴He has worn away my flesh and
my skin,
he has broken my bones;

⁵He has besieged me all around
with poverty and hardship;
⁶He has left me to dwell in dark
places
like those long dead.

⁷He has hemmed me in with no
escape,
weighed me down with chains;
⁸Even when I cry for help,
he stops my prayer;
⁹He has hemmed in my ways with
fitted stones,
and made my paths crooked.

THE VOICE OF A SUFFERING INDIVIDUAL

Lamentations 3:1-66

Chapter 3 differs from the previous two chapters in three ways: First, the acrostic is more defined. In contrast to chapters 1–2, where only the first line of each three-line unit formed the acrostic, in chapter 3 *each* line of each three-*verse* unit begins with the appropriate letter of the alphabet. In several instances two or three lines of the three-verse unit even begin with the same word or root. Secondly, the speaker in verses 1-39 is not Zion portrayed as a woman but is an individual man. There is a transition in verse 40 to a lament of the community. In verse 48 the individual voice returns, although the speaker in verses 52-66 sounds more like the speaker in chapters 1–2, an individual as representative of the whole people. Thirdly, only verses 42-51 seem to have a direct connection to the siege and destruction of Jerusalem in 587 B.C.

Verses 1-25 resemble an individual lament with its accusation of God (3:1-16), description of misery (3:17-20), and turn to hope (3:21-25). Verse 1 presents the topic for the first sixteen verses: "I am one [literally, "a man"; Hebrew *geber*] who has known affliction / under the rod of God's anger." In the next fifteen verses only verse 14 does not have God for the subject. But God does not do what he is expected to do. God leads not to security by springs of water (see Isa 49:10) but into darkness (3:2, 6; see Ps 88:7). God has imprisoned the speaker and blocked off his access even to God (3:5, 7-9). God is a wild animal (3:10-11; see Hos 13:7-8) or a warrior attacking him (3:12-13; see 2:4). God has fed him, not with honey and wheat (see Ps 81:17) nor with blessings (see Jer 31:14) but with bitterness and has broken his teeth with gravel (3:15-16). Oil of wormwood, *Artemesia absin-*

¹⁰He has been a bear lying in wait
for me,
a lion in hiding!
¹¹He turned me aside and tore me
apart,
leaving me ravaged.
¹²He bent his bow, and set me up
as a target for his arrow.

¹³He pierced my kidneys
with shafts from his quiver.
¹⁴I have become a laughingstock to
all my people,
their taunt all day long;
¹⁵He has sated me with bitterness,
filled me with wormwood.

¹⁶He has made me eat gravel,
trampled me into the dust;
¹⁷My life is deprived of peace,
I have forgotten what happiness
is;
¹⁸My enduring hope, I said,
has perished before the LORD.

¹⁹The thought of my wretched
homelessness
is wormwood and poison;
²⁰Remembering it over and over,
my soul is downcast.
²¹But this I will call to mind;
therefore I will hope:

²²The LORD's acts of mercy are not
exhausted,
his compassion is not spent;
²³They are renewed each morning—
great is your faithfulness!
²⁴The LORD is my portion, I tell
myself,
therefore I will hope in him.

²⁵The LORD is good to those who
trust in him,
to the one that seeks him;
²⁶It is good to hope in silence
for the LORD's deliverance.
²⁷It is good for a person, when young,
to bear the yoke,

thium, is bitter. Licking the dust is a common biblical metaphor for humiliation (see Ps 72:9), but here the metaphor is intensified, eating gravel (see Prov 20:17). The description of misery, which was introduced in verse 14, continues in verses 17-20. The speaker is close to despair; his soul is downcast (compare Pss 42:6-7, 12; 43:5).

Like the psalms of lament, this cry to God ends with a turn to hope (3:21-25). These are perhaps the most beautiful verses in this book. Even though God is the one who afflicts, the speaker's hope is grounded in this confession of faith: God's loving compassion does not come to an end (3:22-23). Where else can he go? God is his portion, his lot (3:24). When the land was divided among the tribes, the Levites did not get a share. They were told that the Lord was their portion (Num 18:20; see Josh 18:7). In the psalms the rest of the community claims the Lord as their inherited share (Pss 16:5; 73:26; 119:57; 142:6). Verses 20-22 are striking in their similarity to Psalms 42–43.

3:26-39 A wisdom teaching

The turn to hope leads to a wisdom teaching on perseverance in hope. This instruction is linked to the lament by the catchword, "good." (Throughout this chapter the ideas are not limited to the three-verse alphabetic units.) One can learn to endure suffering (3:26-30) because one hopes in God's enduring

²⁸To sit alone and in silence,
  when its weight lies heavy,
²⁹To put one's mouth in the dust—
  there may yet be hope—
³⁰To offer one's cheek to be struck,
  to be filled with disgrace.

³¹For the Lord does not
  reject forever;
³²Though he brings grief, he takes
    pity,
  according to the abundance of
    his mercy;
³³He does not willingly afflict
  or bring grief to human beings.

³⁴That someone tramples underfoot
  all the prisoners in the land,
³⁵Or denies justice to anyone
  in the very sight of the Most
    High,
³⁶Or subverts a person's lawsuit—
  does the Lord not see?

³⁷Who speaks so that it comes to
    pass,
  unless the Lord commands it?
³⁸Is it not at the word of the Most
    High
  that both good and bad take
    place?
³⁹What should the living complain
    about?
  about their sins!

⁴⁰Let us search and examine our
    ways,
  and return to the LORD!
⁴¹Let us lift up our hearts as well as
    our hands
  toward God in heaven!
⁴²We have rebelled and been
    obstinate;
  you have not forgiven us.

⁴³You wrapped yourself in wrath
    and pursued us,
  killing without pity;

---

love and compassion (3:31-33). God sees the oppression one suffers (3:34-36). There is an echo of Genesis 1 in the recognition that God creates by word (3:37). The ancient idea of causality also appears: if it happened, God did it—whether good or bad (3:38). The implication in these verses is that God has the will and power to save. Therefore it is wise to acknowledge one's own sins, which are the cause of much of one's suffering (3:39). Verse 39 links this section to the beginning with the repetition of *geber*: "What should the living complain about?"

3:40-47 A community lament

The advice to acknowledge and "complain about" one's sins leads to the community's decision to lament (3:40-41). The communal lament, like the individual lament in verses 1-25, begins with an accusation against God (3:42-45). There is a brief confession of sin, but then the complaint begins: "you have not forgiven us." God pursues and kills without pity (3:43; see 2:2, 17, 21). God is wrapped in anger, wrapped in a cloud. The cloud is often a sign of God's presence (see Exod 13:21-22; 24:16-18; 33:9-10; 1 Kgs 8:10-11) but is linked with wrath in the descriptions of the day of the Lord (see Joel 2:2; Zeph 1:15). This time the cloud obscures; God has again blocked himself

⁴⁴You wrapped yourself in a cloud,
   which no prayer could pierce.
⁴⁵You have made us filth and
   rubbish
   among the peoples.

⁴⁶They have opened their mouths
   against us,
   all our enemies;
⁴⁷Panic and the pit have been our
   lot,
   desolation and destruction;
⁴⁸My eyes stream with tears over
   the destruction
   of the daughter of my people.

⁴⁹My eyes will flow without
   ceasing,
   without rest,
⁵⁰Until the LORD from heaven
   looks down and sees.

⁵¹I am tormented by the sight
   of all the daughters of my city.

⁵²Without cause, my enemies
   snared me
   as though I were a bird;
⁵³They tried to end my life in the
   pit,
   pelting me with stones.
⁵⁴The waters flowed over my head:
   and I said, "I am lost!"

⁵⁵I have called upon your name, O
   LORD,
   from the bottom of the pit;
⁵⁶You heard me call, "Do not let
   your ear be deaf
   to my cry for help."
⁵⁷You drew near on the day I called
   you;
   you said, "Do not fear!"

off from the prayer of the people (see 3:8). Without God they are worthless, as good as trash (3:45). Their description of misery (3:46-47) ends with a statement whose alliteration makes it sound like a proverb (*pahad wapahat, hashshe't wehashshaber*, "Panic and pit," "desolation and destruction").

3:48-51 An individual cry

The catchword, "destruction," links the communal lament to the description of agony that follows. In this section the individual voice is again heard. (Note again that this section begins in the middle of a three-verse unit.) The key image in these verses is that of eyes and sight. The word "eyes" appears in three of the four verses; verse 51 begins literally, "my eyes grieve my soul." My eyes are the source of unceasing tears (3:48-49; see Jer 14:17). I plead with God to look at what I cannot bear to see (3:50-51), the suffering in Jerusalem and its surrounding villages. The villages that depend on a city are often called its daughters (see, for example, Judg 11:26).

3:52-66 A partial psalm of thanksgiving

These verses resemble a psalm of thanksgiving with two missing elements: the opening announcement, "I will give thanks," and the concluding promise of a thanksgiving sacrifice. The central part of a thanksgiving psalm is here: description of recent distress (3:52-53), the quotation of the lament (3:54-55), and the announcement that God has heard and acted (3:56-58).

⁵⁸You pleaded my case, Lord,
    you redeemed my life.
⁵⁹You see, LORD, how I am
    wronged;
    do me justice!
⁶⁰You see all their vindictiveness,
    all their plots against me.

⁶¹You hear their reproach, LORD,
    all their plots against me,
⁶²The whispered murmurings of my
    adversaries,
    against me all day long;
⁶³Look! Whether they sit or stand,
    I am the butt of their taunt.

⁶⁴Give them what they deserve,
    LORD,
    according to their deeds;
⁶⁵Give them hardness of heart;
    your curse be upon them;
⁶⁶Pursue them in wrath and destroy
    them
    from under the LORD's heaven!

Miseries of the Besieged City

4 ¹How the gold has lost its luster,
    the noble metal changed;
Jewels lie scattered
    at the corner of every street.

Images of distress echo the psalms—snared by the enemy (3:52; Ps 124:7); in the pit (3:53, 55; Pss 28:1); submerged (3:54; see Ps 69:2). The plea to God and the report of God's action are also reminiscent of psalms: call on the Lord's name (3:55; Ps 116:4); do not be deaf (3:56; see Ps 39:13); you pleaded my case (3:58; Ps 43:1); redeemed my life (3:58; Ps 119:154). God's words in verse 57, "Do not fear," are repeated over and over in prophetic oracles of salvation (for example, Isa 41:13-14).

As the psalms of thanksgiving often do, chapter 3 returns to the lament (3:59-66; see Ps 40). The interpretation of these verses depends on the identification of the speaker. If the speaker is really an individual (perhaps the speaker of vv. 1-25), the enemies seem to be his own people. If the speaker represents the collective voice of Judah (as in chs. 1–2), then the enemies are foreign nations. The accusation against the enemy does not have to do with attack and siege but with plotting, mockery, and injustice (3:59-63). The speaker pleads for retributive justice: do to them what they have done to me (3:64). What the speaker wants done to their hearts in verse 65 is unclear; the Hebrew word occurs only here. It means either "anguish" or "insolence." In any case he wants God to curse them, to pursue them in anger as God has done to him (see 3:43), and to wipe out the sight of them from under the Lord's heaven (see 3:50).

MISERIES OF THE BESIEGED CITY

Lamentations 4:1-22

The pattern of spelling out the alphabet only in the first line of each stanza returns in chapter 4 (see chs. 1–2). The stanzas in this chapter are

²And Zion's precious children,
 worth their weight in gold—
How they are treated like clay jugs,
 the work of any potter!

³Even jackals offer their breasts
 to nurse their young;
But the daughter of my people is as
 cruel
 as the ostrich in the wilderness.

⁴The tongue of the infant cleaves
 to the roof of its mouth in thirst;
Children beg for bread,
 but no one gives them a piece.

⁵Those who feasted on delicacies
 are abandoned in the streets;
Those who reclined on crimson
 now embrace dung heaps.

⁶The punishment of the daughter of
 my people
 surpassed the penalty of Sodom,
Which was overthrown in an
 instant
 with no hand laid on it.

⁷Her princes were brighter than
 snow,
 whiter than milk,
Their bodies more ruddy than coral,
 their beauty like the sapphire.

⁸Now their appearance is blacker
 than soot,
 they go unrecognized in the
 streets;
Their skin has shrunk on their bones,
 and become dry as wood.

---

only two lines each, in contrast to the three-line units in chapters 1–3. Personified Zion does not speak in chapter 4; the only voice is that of the poet who has experienced the siege. Most of the chapter consists of a description of misery; there is no cry to the Lord or petition for help. There is a brief accusation against God and religious leaders (4:11-13), a report of the final days of the siege (4:17-20), and a concluding curse and blessing (4:21-22).

The description of misery (4:1-10, 14-16) lists, group by group, the effects of the siege. Their stories are interwoven. The poet mourns, first of all, that the children of Zion are regarded as worthless (4:1-2). Are the "children" all the people or the young men? The latter is more likely since the women and young children are treated later. The two verses are linked, not only by three different words for "gold" but also by a striking wordplay. "Jewels" are literally "sacred stones"; the Hebrew word for stones (*'abney*) suggests the word for "children" in the next verse (*beney*). The children of Zion are holy and precious as jewels, but they lie starving or dead at the corner of every street (see 2:19).

The little children and their mothers suffer desperately from the famine resulting from the siege (4:3-4). The starving mothers cannot nurse and so the children starve. The mothers are scorned as cruel by contrast to the most despised animals. The ostrich was widely believed to lay her eggs in the desert sand and then abandon them. Jackals and ostriches live in ruins and deserted places (Isa 34:13), a foreshadowing of what Jerusalem will become, and are associated with lamentation (Mic 1:8).

⁹Better for those pierced by the
sword
than for those pierced by
hunger,
Better for those who bleed from
wounds
than for those who lack food.

¹⁰The hands of compassionate
women
have boiled their own children!
They became their food
when the daughter of my
people was shattered.

¹¹The LORD has exhausted his anger,
poured out his blazing wrath;

He has kindled a fire in Zion
that has consumed her
foundations.

¹²The kings of the earth did not
believe,
nor any of the world's
inhabitants,
That foe or enemy could enter
the gates of Jerusalem.

¹³Except for the sins of her prophets
and the crimes of her priests,
Who poured out in her midst
the blood of the just.

¹⁴They staggered blindly in the
streets,
defiled with blood,

Verse 5 moves from the image of starving children to a description of the starving rich. Those who not only had enough to eat but who ate delicacies now starve with everyone else; those who were comfortable on fine furniture now pick through the trash. Crimson (or purple) is a sign of wealth because the dye was difficult to obtain; only the wealthy could afford it. This image of the pampered rich leads to a reflection on Daughter Zion (4:6). This is the only suggestion of guilt in this chapter. The contrast drawn is stunning: Zion must be *more* guilty than Sodom because her suffering is long and drawn out. Sodom and Gomorrah (see Gen 19) are metaphors for great guilt and destruction. The prophets accuse the people of being *as* guilty as Sodom (see Jer 23:14) but not *more* guilty. They warn of total destruction like Sodom's (see Isa 1:9; Jer 49:18; 50:40); is there a threat to Jerusalem here?

The poet begins again with the same groups—men, women, and children, those whose suffering is long—but the description is intensified. The starving men are princes (4:7). (Or, since the Hebrew word is *nazir*, they may be Nazirites who have made special promises to God; see Num 6.) The praise of their beauty recalls descriptions of David and the lover in the Song of Songs (see 1 Sam 16:12; Song 5:10-16). But now they are disfigured by starvation (4:8). A proverbial sentence recalls the comparison of Sodom and Zion: It is better to die quickly than to suffer long (4:9). As for the starving women and children, the ravages of famine lead mothers to cannibalism (4:10). Cannibalism is reported as a result of siege in 2 Kings (6:28-29); the prophets threaten that it will come even to Jerusalem (Jer 19:8-9; Ezek 5:10).

So that people could not touch
even their garments:

¹⁵"Go away! Unclean!" they cried to
them,
"Away, away, do not touch!"
If they went away and wandered,
it would be said among the
nations,
"They can no longer live here!"

¹⁶The presence of the LORD was
their portion,
but he no longer looks upon
them.

The priests are shown no regard,
the elders, no mercy.

¹⁷Even now our eyes are worn out,
searching in vain for help;
From our watchtower we have
watched
for a nation unable to save.

¹⁸They dogged our every step,
we could not walk in our
squares;
Our end drew near, our time was
up;
yes, our end had come.

The Lord, who has not yet been mentioned in chapter 4, is now accused of bringing this disaster on Zion (4:11). The disaster is so great that not even foreign nations can believe it (4:12). There is an implied contrast with Psalm 48: "See! The kings assembled, / together they advanced. / When they looked they were astounded; / terrified, they were put to flight!" (Ps 48:5-6). A tradition had grown up around Zion that it could not be defeated. The Assyrian king, Sennacherib, could not conquer it at the end of the eighth century (2 Kgs 19:32-36); the psalms declare the invulnerability of the city (Ps 46:5-8). Jeremiah warned, however, that what protected Zion was not the presence of the temple but the presence of God, and God would remain with the people only if they were faithful to the covenant (Jer 7). Ezekiel reports the departure of God from the temple (Ezek 10:18-23).

Verse 13 is incomplete. What happens because of the sins of the religious leaders? Genuine prophets describe the sins of false prophets and priests and their consequences: Priests have rejected knowledge and ignored God's law (Hos 4:4-9). Prophets speak peace to those who feed them and war to those who do not (Mic 3:5). Priests did not seek God; prophets prophesied by idols (Jer 2:8). Therefore the people come to ruin and Jerusalem will be destroyed (Mic 3:12).

Verses 14-16 complete the description of misery by portraying the agony of priests and elders. They, who guarded the sanctuary, now cannot enter it because they are defiled by blood (4:14). Are they simply bloody from the surrounding warfare? This ordinarily would not render them unclean. Or are they guilty of bloodshed because they did not care for the vulnerable in their midst (see Isa 1:15-17)? In Isaiah God says to such people: "Trample my courts no more!" (Isa 1:13-14). They cry out like a leper (Lev 13:45-46)

¹⁹Our pursuers were swifter
than eagles in the sky,
In the mountains they were hot on
our trail,
they ambushed us in the
wilderness.

²⁰The LORD's anointed—our very
lifebreath!—
was caught in their snares,
He in whose shade we thought
to live among the nations.

²¹Rejoice and gloat, daughter Edom,
dwelling in the land of Uz,
The cup will pass to you as well;
you shall become drunk and
strip yourself naked!

²²Your punishment is completed,
daughter Zion,
the Lord will not prolong your
exile;
The Lord will punish your iniquity,
daughter Edom,
will lay bare your sins.

---

and are shunned even among the nations (4:15). The presence of God was their portion (4:16; see 3:24). Now, since God's face (i.e., presence) is not with them, their faces are not lifted up (i.e., they are not honored).

4:17-20 Jerusalem's fall

The tone changes in the next section. It seems to be a detailed report of the final days of Jerusalem. Similar reports from Jeremiah and 2 Kings help explain these verses. Jerusalem had trusted in Egypt to defend it against the Babylonians (see Jer 37:1-10), but Egypt did not come (4:17). The city walls were breached on the ninth day of the fourth month and the people could no longer walk in the streets (4:18; see 2 Kgs 25:3-4). King Zedekiah and his soldiers left the city by night, "But the Chaldean [Babylonian] army pursued the king and overtook him in the desert near Jericho" (2 Kgs 25:5; see 4:19-20). Like every king of Judah, Zedekiah was anointed, and thus "messiah"; the Hebrew word for "anointed" is *mashiach*. The hopes for every "messiah" are reflected in the way he is named: "lifebreath" and protecting "shade" (see Ps 72). Now that hope is shattered also.

4:21-22 A curse

The last two verses of the chapter are a curse on Edom and a statement of renewed hope for Zion. Edom (another name for Esau), Judah's neighbor to the south, was considered a brother to Israel/Jacob (see Gen 25:30; 32:29). When the Babylonians conquered and destroyed Jerusalem in 587 B.C., the Edomites joined in the pillage. For this they were bitterly hated (Obad 10–14). The poet taunts Edom, in effect saying: "Rejoice now, but your day is coming." The cup of God's wrath is a common prophetic image (see Isa 51:17; Jer 25:15-17). Drunken Edom will be stripped bare—the fate they called down on Jerusalem (Ps 137:7)—and its sins revealed (4:22). For Zion, however, there is hope. From the vantage point of the future, the poet pro-

"Our pursuers were swifter than eagles in the sky" (Lam 4:19).

The Community's Lament to the Lord

5 ¹Remember, LORD, what has happened to us,
  pay attention, and see our
    disgrace:
²Our heritage is turned over to
    strangers,
  our homes, to foreigners.
³We have become orphans, without
    fathers;
  our mothers are like widows.
⁴We pay money to drink our own
    water,
  our own wood comes at a price.
⁵With a yoke on our necks, we are
    driven;
  we are worn out, but allowed no
    rest.

⁶We extended a hand to Egypt and
    Assyria,
  to satisfy our need of bread.
⁷Our ancestors, who sinned, are no
    more;
  but now we bear their guilt.
⁸Servants rule over us,
  with no one to tear us from their
    hands.
⁹We risk our lives just to get bread,
  exposed to the desert heat;
¹⁰Our skin heats up like an oven,
  from the searing blasts of famine.

¹¹Women are raped in Zion,
  young women in the cities of
    Judah;
¹²Princes have been hanged by them,
  elders shown no respect.

claims that her punishment is complete, a promise announced by Isaiah of the exile: "Speak to the heart of Jerusalem, and proclaim to her / that her service has ended, / that her guilt is expiated, / That she has received from the hand of the LORD / double for all her sins" (Isa 40:2).

THE COMMUNITY'S LAMENT TO THE LORD

Lamentations 5:1-22

Lamentations 5 differs from the other chapters in several ways: First, there is no acrostic; the first letters of each line do not spell the alphabet. There are, however, twenty-two lines, recalling the twenty-two letters of the alphabet. Second, each verse has only one line instead of three (chs. 1–2) or two (ch. 3). Third, the meter of the lines is not predominantly 3 + 2 (the *qinah* rhythm; see Introduction) but primarily 3 + 3. Fourth, this chapter fits most closely the pattern and style of the communal lament in the psalms. There is a cry to God, a description of distress, a complaint, and an appeal for help. The turn to hope, however, is very slight if it is there at all. This similarity to the psalms may be the reason chapter 5 has the heading in some Greek and Latin manuscripts: "A Prayer (or Lament) of Jeremiah."

The chapter is framed by two cries to God (5:1, 21). The cry to God in verse 1 is similar to the cry in other chapters (see 1:9, 11; 2:20). But here the people plead with God not only to look but also to remember. Remembering in Hebrew has the connotation of actively making something present.

13Young men carry millstones,
  boys stagger under loads of
     wood;
14The elders have abandoned the
     gate,
  the young men their music.

15The joy of our hearts has ceased,
  dancing has turned into
     mourning;

16The crown has fallen from our
     head:
  woe to us that we sinned!
17Because of this our hearts grow
     sick,
  at this our eyes grow dim:
18Because of Mount Zion, lying
     desolate,
  and the jackals roaming there!

God is asked to take their misery to heart. A major part of their distress in this shame-honor culture is the disgrace they have suffered.

Several elements in this chapter, including the cry to God to remember, suggest Psalm 74, a communal lament over an enemy invasion of the temple (Ps 74:2, 18, 22). Other similarities are: the questions "why" and "how long" (5:20; Ps 74:1, 10-11); the description of the desolation of Mount Zion (5:18; Ps 74:3-7); the plea for restoration (5:21; Ps 74:21); the absence of praise or thanksgiving at the end (5:22; Ps 74:22-23).

5:2-18 A description of distress

Strangers have taken over the land. "Heritage" may mean the whole land (see Num 26:52-56) or it may connote one's individual piece of land (see Judg 2:6). A share in the land is part of the covenant promise (see Gen 12:7; Deut 11:8-9). For this reason Naboth refuses to give his vineyard to King Ahab in the ninth century (1 Kgs 21:1-3). Loss of the land is seen as loss of the covenant. Therefore, the people regard themselves as fatherless (5:3).

Foreign domination also has practical consequences. What once belonged to them they must now buy (5:4). They suffer forced labor without profit (5:5). They are reduced to begging relief from other nations (5:6). "Wood" and "water" (5:4) signify all material needs. "Rest" (5:5) suggests again the loss of the covenant promise, "rest" in the land (see Deut 12:10).

An acknowledgment of guilt interrupts the description of distress (5:7). It is the familiar refrain of suffering for the guilt of ancestors (see Ezek 18); later the people will also bemoan their own sins (5:16). The "sins" may be the foreign alliances with Egypt and Assyria (see Isa 8:11-15; 30:1-5; Jer 2:18-19).

The description of distress resumes with a repetition of previous complaints (4:8-9). "Servants," the administrators of the Babylonians, rule them. They not only have to work and to buy what was their own, but they still suffer from famine (5:10). The suffering of various groups of people mentioned in chapter 4 is again described (5:11-13). Even the young men, the

¹⁹But you, LORD, are enthroned
forever;
your throne stands from age to
age.
²⁰Why have you utterly forgotten
us,
forsaken us for so long?

²¹Bring us back to you, LORD, that
we may return:
renew our days as of old.
²²For now you have indeed rejected
us
and utterly turned your wrath
against us.

---

people's hope, are forced to do "women's work," grinding grain (v. 13). Joy has departed (5:14-17).

5:18-22 A turn to hope?

The last five verses swing between misery and hope. The sanctuary has been desecrated; Mount Zion has become the haunt of wild animals as the prophets warned (see Jer 9:10; 10:22). But the Lord, not dependent on any place, is enthroned forever (5:19; see Pss 55:20; 102:13). This tiny hymn fragment is as close as this chapter comes to a turn to hope. But immediately the lament returns with its age-old questions: Why? How long? (see Pss 42:10; 79:10; 80:5; 94:3). A second plea to God rings out (v. 21; see 5:1). There are two requests: bring us back, renew us. (The first half of the verse is an almost direct quotation of Jer 31:18.) In chapter 3 the people had resolved to return to the Lord (3:40); here they recognize that they cannot return under their own power. Only God can bring them back (see Jer 31:18; Ps 51:12). Zion and its people have been looking for renewal and revival throughout the book. In chapter 1 the people tried to revive their own lives and Zion tried to find renewal through others (1:11, 16), but neither was successful. In chapter 3 the speaker declared his hope in God's loving mercy, renewed each morning (3:22-23). Now the people beg God to renew them.

This lament does not end with thanksgiving or praise of God for rescue. Instead, like Psalm 88, Lamentations 5 says to God, "Now it's your turn to act." Verse 22 is, in effect, an accusation against God: "We are still suffering and it's your fault." The accusation itself is an expression of faith, recognition that no one but God can relieve this misery. So ends the book of Lamentations.

Ecclesiastes

Name and attribution

The book of Ecclesiastes begins with a typical introduction of the speaker: "The words of So-and-So, son of So-and-So" (see Jer 1:1; Amos 1:1; Prov 30:1; Neh 1:1). The speaker's name is "Qoheleth," a word that appears only in this book in the Hebrew Bible (1:2, 12; 7:27; 12:8-10). The term is a feminine participle of the verb *qahal*, which means "to assemble or gather." (The feminine form is often used for an official status.) The related noun is the term for the gathered assembly of Israel. So Qoheleth is a gatherer or collector, whether of people or of wise sayings. In Greek the assembly is *ekklesia*, and the gatherer or member of the assembly is *ekklesiastes* (in Latin *ecclesiastes*). Thus the book is often named "Ecclesiastes." Because of the connection to the liturgical assembly, Luther interpreted the name to mean "The Preacher."

Qoheleth is identified as "David's son . . . king in Jerusalem." In 1:12, he claims to have been "king over Israel." So the speaker takes on the persona of Solomon, the only one of David's sons who ruled over all twelve tribes and could thus be called "king of Israel." Solomon (a collector of women, wealth, and wisdom) is the patron of biblical wisdom. When God offered to give him whatever he asked, he asked for wisdom, "a listening heart" (1 Kgs 3:9). Solomon was said to have greater wisdom than all the sages of the East (1 Kgs 5:10-14). Even the Queen of Sheba came to test his wisdom (1 Kgs 10:1-10). The book of Proverbs is put under his patronage (Prov 1:1). Song of Songs and the Wisdom of Solomon are written under his name. This book too, which challenges traditional wisdom, is given legitimacy by the claim of Solomonic authorship.

Date and authorship

Two clues help in the dating of Ecclesiastes: the form of Hebrew used (characteristic of the fifth century B.C. or later) and the presence of fragments of two manuscripts of the book among the Dead Sea Scrolls (which puts it earlier than the second century B.C.). The date confirms the fact that Solomon, who lived in the tenth century, is not the author. The author is a sage, probably also a teacher (see 12:9), living and writing in the environs of Jerusalem.

Structure

The book begins with a title (1:1) and ends with an epilogue (12:9-14), both written by a later editor. The turning point, exactly halfway through the book with 111 verses before and after it, is between 6:8 and 6:9. Beyond these observations, there is no agreement on the structure. The first half is characterized by the refrain "a chase after wind." The second half repeats the ideas of knowing/not knowing and finding/not finding.

Key concepts

The best-known word in Ecclesiastes is "vanity" (*hebel*), which occurs thirty-eight times in the book. The word means "vapor" or "puff of wind" and connotes futility, absurdity, unreliability. The repetition of the word in 1:2 and 12:8 sets the tone for this work. Another key concept is "profit" or "gain." Qoheleth, in the voice of an accountant, keeps asking of every human action, "What do we gain?" The reason that nothing is profitable is a third theme: death. At the time when this book was written there was no belief in meaningful life after death. So whatever humans do, death wipes out in the end. The view that this life is all there is leads to another preoccupation of Qoheleth, the unfairness of life. The just suffer and the wicked prosper; all is vanity!

Qoheleth's view of life is not unrelieved darkness, however. In his meditation on time he concludes that human beings cannot understand the proper time for things, but they can take hold of the present moment. Seven times he repeats the advice to enjoy the present moment because it is a gift of God (2:24-26; 3:12-13, 22; 5:17-19; 8:15; 9:7-10; 11:9-10). This advice (echoed almost exactly in 9:7-9) is found already in the third-millennium story of the Mesopotamian hero Gilgamesh, who goes off in search of immortality.

Qoheleth describes God as the one in control of all that happens and active in every event. Human beings can neither understand nor change God, so Qoheleth advises that fearing God is the best course of action. The term used to name God is Elohim, the generic word for "god"; the personal name of God, YHWH, is never used.

How to read

On the one hand, the statements in this book seem straightforward and obvious. Certainly we work hard and then everything goes to someone else (2:18-23)! On the other hand, the book is full of contradictions. Wisdom is better than folly, but "in much wisdom is much sorrow" (1:18; 2:13). "[T]here is nothing better than to be glad and to do well during life," but "[t]he heart of the wise is in the house of mourning" (3:12; 7:4). The reader is encouraged to notice the contradictions and to relish them. Is human life not contradictory?

Ecclesiastes

1 ¹The words of David's son, Qoheleth, king in Jerusalem:

²Vanity of vanities, says Qoheleth,
    vanity of vanities! All things are
        vanity!

Vanity of Human Toil

³What profit have we from all the toil
    which we toil at under the sun?

⁴One generation departs and
    another generation comes,
        but the world forever stays.
⁵The sun rises and the sun sets;
    then it presses on to the place
        where it rises.
⁶Shifting south, then north,
    back and forth shifts the wind,
        constantly shifting its
            course.

SETTING THE THEME

Ecclesiastes 1:1-11

After the title (1:1), verse 2 presents the theme of the book: "All things are vanity!" "Vanity" (*hebel*) is repeated six times in this verse (see Introduction). The phrase "X of X" is the Hebrew way of expressing a superlative, the "highest vanity." Over and over Qoheleth will demonstrate that human experience and knowledge, even human life itself, are fleeting and insubstantial. Human beings cannot cling to any moment, nor can they fully understand even themselves. "Every man is but a breath" (Ps 39:6, 12; see Pss 62:10; 144:4). Verse 2 is repeated at the end of the book (12:8), forming an inclusion (the same phrases or words repeated at beginning and end) and is echoed throughout the book.

1:3-11 Vanity of human toil

The futility of human toil is presented first in a poem (1:3-8) and then in a prose commentary (1:9-11). There is no profit in all this human striving. The word "profit" (or "advantage") occurs ten times in the book; it means the surplus created by human effort. "Under the sun," a phrase that occurs twenty-nine times in Qoheleth and nowhere else in the Hebrew Bible, means "during this earthly life." In Qoheleth's time it was believed that at death

"The sun rises and the sun sets; then it presses on to the place where it rises" (Eccl 1:5).

⁷All rivers flow to the sea,
    yet never does the sea become
        full.
To the place where they flow,
    the rivers continue to flow.
⁸All things are wearisome,
    too wearisome for words.
The eye is not satisfied by seeing
    nor has the ear enough of
        hearing.

⁹What has been, that will be; what has been done, that will be done. Nothing is new under the sun! ¹⁰Even the thing of which we say, "See, this is new!" has already existed in the ages that preceded us. ¹¹There is no remembrance of past generations; nor will future generations be remembered by those who come after them.

I. Qoheleth's Investigation of Life

Twofold Introduction. ¹²I, Qoheleth, was king over Israel in Jerusalem, ¹³and I applied my mind to search and investigate in wisdom all things that are done under the sun.

A bad business God has given
    to human beings to be busied
        with.

---

persons left the sunlight and entered into the silent darkness of a place called Sheol. Meanwhile, in human experience before death everything keeps running in its same course. Generation replaces generation. Every night the sun has to race (literally "pant") to get back to the place it began the previous morning. The winds have their regular cycle, and, for all their flowing, the rivers never produce more water. There is no profit! The same holds true for human desire: everything makes us tired, yet we are never satisfied. The prose commentary explains: Nothing new will ever happen; even what is past—people or events—is soon forgotten.

QOHELETH'S INVESTIGATION OF LIFE

Ecclesiastes 1:12–6:9

1:12-18 Twofold introduction

After his self-introduction, Qoheleth describes his experience, supporting his conclusions with proverbs. Even wisdom does not profit! God appears here for the first time in the book: Qoheleth concludes that God has set humans to a worthless task (1:13). The refrain that characterizes the first half of the book also appears for the first time: "all is vanity and a chase after wind" (1:14; see 2:11, 17, 26; 4:4, 16; 6:9). The word translated "chase" is related to "shepherd"; in vain does one "shepherd the wind." Chasing the wind is characteristic of a fool (see Sir 34:1-2). A proverb states the reason that even through wisdom one cannot acquire full knowledge. The implied actor is God: What God has made crooked, human beings cannot make straight (1:15; see 7:13). The first line of the proverb suggests ancient Near

¹⁴I have seen all things that are done under the sun, and behold, all is vanity and a chase after wind.

¹⁵What is crooked cannot be made straight,
and you cannot count what is not there.

¹⁶Though I said to myself, "See, I have greatly increased my wisdom beyond all who were before me in Jerusalem, and my mind has broad experience of wisdom and knowledge," ¹⁷yet when I applied my mind to know wisdom and knowledge, madness and folly, I learned that this also is a chase after wind.

¹⁸For in much wisdom there is much sorrow;
whoever increases knowledge increases grief.

2 **Study of Pleasure-seeking.** ¹I said in my heart, "Come, now, let me try you with pleasure and the enjoyment of good things." See, this too was vanity. ²Of laughter I said: "Mad!" and of mirth: "What good does this do?" ³Guided by wisdom, I probed with my mind how to beguile my senses with wine and take up folly, until I should understand what is good for human beings to do under the heavens during the limited days of their lives.

⁴I undertook great works; I built myself houses and planted vineyards; ⁵I made gardens and parks, and in them set out fruit trees of all sorts. ⁶And I constructed for myself reservoirs to water a flourishing woodland. ⁷I acquired male and female slaves, and had slaves who were born in my house. I also owned

Eastern ideas concerning the purpose of education: to make stubborn students (the crooked) straight. Qoheleth says that not only does this not work in education, it is impossible in any other toil. The second metaphor is economic: What is lacking, one cannot count. The term, "lacking" (NABRE: "what is not there"), suggests the phrase from Psalm 23: "there is nothing I lack." Qoheleth says human beings do indeed lack, and what is lacking is understanding of what exists.

Qoheleth begins again by stating his qualifications for this search for understanding (1:16). His statement recalls the description of Solomon (1 Kgs 5:9-11). He expands his search to include wisdom's opposite, striving to understand by circling to the other side: madness and folly (1:17). This too is shepherding the wind. It is common knowledge that to acquire wisdom one may have to suffer (no pain; no gain), but Qoheleth's proverb declares that wisdom itself is a cause of pain and grief (1:18). In this introductory section Qoheleth turns traditional wisdom on its head: wisdom itself is futile!

2:1-17 Study of pleasure-seeking

Chapter 2 is divided into three sections by the refrain, "All is vanity and a chase after wind" (2:11, 17, 26). The word "vanity" appears eight times

vast herds of cattle and flocks of sheep, more than all who had been before me in Jerusalem. [8]I amassed for myself silver and gold, and the treasures of kings and provinces. I provided for myself male and female singers and delights of men, many women. [9]I accumulated much more than all others before me in Jerusalem; my wisdom, too, stayed with me. [10]Nothing that my eyes desired did I deny them, nor did I deprive myself of any joy; rather, my heart rejoiced in the fruit of all my toil. This was my share for all my toil. [11]But when I turned to all the works that my hands had wrought, and to the fruit of the toil for which I had toiled so much, see! all was vanity and a chase after wind. There is no profit under the sun. [12]What about one who succeeds a king? He can do only what has already been done.

Study of Wisdom and Folly. I went on to the consideration of wisdom, madness and folly. [13]And I saw that wisdom has as much profit over folly as light has over darkness.

[14]Wise people have eyes in their
heads,
but fools walk in darkness.

Yet I knew that the same lot befalls both. [15]So I said in my heart, if the fool's

---

in this chapter (2:1, 11, 15, 17, 19, 21, 23, 26). Qoheleth is setting out "to know wisdom and knowledge, madness and folly" (1:17), but his move to specific experiences in chapter 2 shows that his quest is indeed vain!

The first area of Qoheleth's quest is pleasure (2:1-11). After testing merriment and intoxication (2:2-3), he moves to the pleasure of great accomplishments (2:4-6). Two of these verses begin with "I made/constructed" (2:5, 6; see also 2:8b). Qoheleth's list of great works recalls other descriptions of Solomon's accomplishments: palaces and vineyards (1 Kgs 3:1; 10:4; see Song 8:11), gardens and parks (Neh 2:8; 3:15), reservoirs and forests (Neh 2:14). The remains of three reservoirs south of Jerusalem are still known as Solomon's pools; the name comes from a first-century historian, Josephus (*Antiquities of the Jews* 8.186). Qoheleth also acquires everything his heart desires: slaves, livestock, wealth, and entertainers (2:7-9). This too recalls Solomon, who was known as the richest king in Israel and who had seven hundred wives and three hundred concubines (1 Kgs 10:23; 11:3). Despite the abundance, the only possible gain of this quest is delight in the toil itself (2:10). But even that is vanity; there is no profit (2:11).

Verse 12 is not clear in Hebrew. The NABRE has reversed the two halves of the verse and added the phrase "He can do only." The second half of the verse (first in NABRE) introduces the subject of the king's successor (see also 2:16, 18-19). He too can do nothing new. The first half of the verse (second in NABRE) reiterates the general subject of Qoheleth's quest—wisdom, madness, and folly (see 1:17).

lot is to befall me also, why should I be wise? Where is the profit? And in my heart I decided that this too is vanity. [16]The wise person will have no more abiding remembrance than the fool; for in days to come both will have been forgotten. How is it that the wise person dies like the fool! [17]Therefore I detested life, since for me the work that is done under the sun is bad; for all is vanity and a chase after wind.

Study of the Fruits of Toil

To Others the Profits. [18]And I detested all the fruits of my toil under the sun, because I must leave them to the one who is to come after me. [19]And who knows whether that one will be wise or a fool? Yet that one will take control of all the fruits of my toil and wisdom under the sun. This also is vanity. [20]So my heart turned to despair over all the fruits of my toil under the sun. [21]For here

---

2:13-17 Study of wisdom and folly

In the next section, Qoheleth turns to wisdom itself and its opposite, folly. "Wisdom/wise" and "folly/fool" appear in every verse in this section except the last. Qoheleth's first conclusion is that here, finally, there is "profit." There is more gain in wisdom than in folly (2:13). This gain is overwhelming—as much as light over darkness. Light and darkness are often symbols of life and death. The difference between wisdom and folly is as great as the difference between life and death. Since the goal of wisdom is always the good life, this statement seems obvious. Qoheleth even supports it with a proverb (2:14). But this happy assertion collapses with the observation that both the wise and fools die. Death wipes out all "profit"— even the profit of wisdom (2:15).

When this book was written there was no belief in any meaningful life after death. All the dead were thought to go to a place called Sheol where there was no joy, no feeling, no communication, no memory. It was even debated whether God could be present in Sheol (compare Ps 88:11-13 with Ps 139:8). The only hope for immortality was through one's children and through being remembered. Even this, says Qoheleth, is vanity. Even the hope for immortality through being remembered is futile. Everyone is forgotten in death (2:16). The result of Qoheleth's quest is hatred for life (2:17).

2:18-26 Study of the fruits of toil

In verse 10 Qoheleth rejoiced in the fruit of his toil; in this third section he seeks the "profit" in toil. This quest too leads to despair, because whatever one has gained has to be left to one's heirs at death. The heir, who has not earned this gain, may be a fool. So not only is there no hope for immortality through one's children, there is not even the hope that what little one has gained through wisdom will be used wisely. No wonder Qoheleth

is one who has toiled with wisdom and knowledge and skill, and that one's legacy must be left to another who has not toiled for it. This also is vanity and a great evil. ²²For what profit comes to mortals from all the toil and anxiety of heart with which they toil under the sun? ²³Every day sorrow and grief are their occupation; even at night their hearts are not at rest. This also is vanity.

²⁴There is nothing better for mortals than to eat and drink and provide themselves with good things from their toil. Even this, I saw, is from the hand of God. ²⁵For who can eat or drink apart from God? ²⁶For to the one who pleases God, he gives wisdom and knowledge and joy; but to the one who displeases, God gives the task of gathering possessions for the one who pleases God. This also is vanity and a chase after wind.

No One Can Determine the Right Time To Act

3 ¹There is an appointed time for everything,
and a time for every affair under the heavens.
²A time to give birth, and a time to die;
a time to plant, and a time to uproot the plant.
³A time to kill, and a time to heal;
a time to tear down, and a time to build.
⁴A time to weep, and a time to laugh;
a time to mourn, and a time to dance.

---

despairs! Why should people work so hard? There is no profit; there is only grief (2:22-23).

The chapter closes with a slight glimmer of hope. The future holds no promise, but there is still the present. Verses 24-25 introduce an idea that will thread throughout the book: the present moment, with its joys and sorrows, is a gift from God. It is all that mortals have, and so there is nothing better than to enjoy it.

3:1-15 No one can determine the right time to act

The opening poem (3:1-8) is perhaps the best-known passage in Qoheleth, but without its prose commentary (3:9-15) it is easily misunderstood. The poem is a beautiful meditation on the proper time for everything in human life from birth to death. Each line sets out opposite experiences and each verse (with the possible exception of 3:5) has an inner parallelism. For example, seeking is opposed to losing, but seeking is related to keeping and losing to casting away (3:6). Verse 2 opposes *giving* birth (not "being born") to dying; thus it parallels planting and uprooting. Various interpretations are given for verse 5a. Does scattering and gathering stones refer to counting, buying, and selling (see Deut 25:13, where the "weights" are literally "stones")? Does it relate to building fences and setting boundaries (see Gen 31:46-52)? Is it a sexual reference (see Exod 1:16, where the midwives

⁵A time to scatter stones, and a time to gather them;
a time to embrace, and a time to be far from embraces.
⁶A time to seek, and a time to lose;
a time to keep, and a time to cast away.
⁷A time to rend, and a time to sew;
a time to be silent, and a time to speak.
⁸A time to love, and a time to hate;
a time of war, and a time of peace.
⁹What profit have workers from their toil? ¹⁰I have seen the business that God has given to mortals to be busied about.

¹¹God has made everything appropriate to its time, but has put the timeless into their hearts so they cannot find out, from beginning to end, the work which God has done. ¹²I recognized that there is nothing better than to rejoice and to do well during life. ¹³Moreover, that all can eat and drink and enjoy the good of all their toil—this is a gift of God. ¹⁴I recognized that whatever God does will endure forever; there is no adding to it, or taking from it. Thus has God done that he may be revered. ¹⁵What now is has already been; what is to be, already is: God retrieves what has gone by.

are supposed to look at the "stones" /balls to determine the gender of the baby)? This last interpretation would parallel the second half of the verse. The final verse of the poem (3:9) reverses the parallelism—love (A), hate (B), war (B'), peace (A')—thus ending the poem on a positive note. The mirroring pattern (ABBA), called chiasm, is a common technique in Hebrew poetry.

The prose commentary (3:9-15) returns to the problems of chapter 1: what profit (3:9; see 1:3), a bad business (3:10; see 1:13). Chapter 3 began with the statement that "there is an appointed time for everything." God has set this "appointed time," but human beings cannot find it. God has put "the timeless" into human hearts, but they cannot understand what God has done (3:11). The "timeless" (Hebrew, *'olam*), connotes a long time, or the distant past, or forever. The hunger for more than the present (the timeless) is planted in human hearts, but human experience is caught in this rhythm of events one after the other (within time). A characteristic of the wise, according to the rest of wisdom literature, is that they know the proper time (see, e.g., Prov 25:11; Sir 20:5-6; 51:30). In the midst of this ambiguity between time and the timeless, Qoheleth knows only two things, one about God's work and the other about human response. How human beings should respond has been stated before: enjoy the present moment; it is God's gift (3:12-13; see 2:24-26). Regarding God's work, it lasts forever; human understanding cannot grasp its immensity. What humans cannot hold onto, God retrieves. (Literally, "God seeks what was pursued"—the chase after wind?) The awareness that God is beyond human understanding leads to awe and fear of the Lord, the beginning of wisdom (3:14-15).

respect

The Problem of Retribution. [16]And still under the sun in the judgment place I saw wickedness, and wickedness also in the seat of justice. [17]I said in my heart, both the just and the wicked God will judge, since a time is set for every affair and for every work. [18]I said in my heart: As for human beings, it is God's way of testing them and of showing that they are in themselves like beasts. [19]For the lot of mortals and the lot of beasts is the same lot: The one dies as well as the other. Both have the same life breath. Human beings have no advantage over beasts, but all is vanity. [20]Both go to the same place; both were made from the dust, and to the dust they both return.

[21]Who knows if the life breath of mortals goes upward and the life breath of beasts goes earthward? [22]And I saw that there is nothing better for mortals than to rejoice in their work; for this is their lot. Who will let them see what is to come after them?

Vanity of Toil. [1]Again I saw all the oppressions that take place under the sun: the tears of the victims with none to comfort them! From the hand of their oppressors comes violence, and there is none to comfort them! [2]And those now dead, I declared more fortunate in death than are the living to be still alive. [3]And better off than both is the yet unborn, who has not seen the wicked work that

3:16-22 Problem of retribution

Qoheleth observes that life is not fair (3:16). Only God can judge with justice, because only God knows the appropriate time (3:17). Human beings are humbled because they cannot see as God sees (3:18). They are mortal like the animals. Both die; both return to the dust from which they were made (3:19-20; see Job 34:14-15; Ps 104:29). Qoheleth puzzles over where the "life-breath" goes. Does the breath of humans return to God (3:21)? It must be remembered that Qoheleth does not have a belief in meaningful life after death. Neither God's judgment of people nor the question about life-breath implies human immortality. Qoheleth knows simply that God is the only one who has power to judge and to give and take life. He concludes again that the only hope for mortals is in the present moment (3:22).

4:1-6 Vanity of toil

After declaring that there is "nothing better" for mortals than to rejoice now in their work (3:22), Qoheleth continues with two "better" sayings. Such sayings—this is better than that—are common in wisdom literature (e.g., Prov 15:16-17; 17:1; Sir 20:31). Having observed that life is unfair (3:16), he turns his attention to those who suffer violence (4:1). Twice he declares that "there is none to comfort them" (see Lam 1). So the dead who no longer suffer are more fortunate than the living, and the unborn better off than either (4:2-3). When he considers work, Qoheleth sees that all human accomplishments come out of competition (4:4). The observation is followed

Only hope of mortals is in the present moment

is done under the sun. ⁴Then I saw that all toil and skillful work is the rivalry of one person with another. This also is vanity and a chase after wind.

⁵"Fools fold their arms
    and consume their own flesh"—
⁶Better is one handful with
        tranquility
    than two with toil and a chase
            after wind!

Companions and Successors. ⁷Again I saw this vanity under the sun: ⁸those all alone with no companion, with neither child nor sibling—with no end to all their toil, and no satisfaction from riches. For whom do I toil and deprive myself of good things? This also is vanity and a bad business. ⁹Two are better than one: They get a good wage for their toil. ¹⁰If the one falls, the other will help the fallen one. But woe to the solitary person! If that one should fall, there is no other to help. ¹¹So also, if two sleep together, they keep each other warm. How can one alone keep warm? ¹²Where one alone may be overcome, two together can resist. A three-ply cord is not easily broken.

¹³Better is a poor but wise youth than an old but foolish king who no longer knows caution; ¹⁴for from a prison house he came forth to reign; despite his kingship he was born poor. ¹⁵I saw all the living, those who move about under the sun,

by two proverbial sayings, seemingly opposed to one another. Fools, who "fold their arms" and thus do no work, will starve to death ("consume their own flesh"). On the other hand, it is better to have little without worry than to work oneself to death, chasing the wind (4:5-6)! This last saying echoes the repeated advice to enjoy the present moment.

4:7-16 Companions and successors

Verses 7-8, at the center of chapter 4, link the preceding advice concerning overwork with the following "better" saying (4:9). Not only is it a "bad business" to spend all one's energy on work and never be satisfied, it is even worse if there is no one with whom one can or does share the results. (See Sirach's words against the miser: If ever he is generous, "it is by mistake"; 14:7.)

Several reasons are given that "two are better than one" (4:9-12). Living is more economical for two; one can help the other in trouble. They warm each other in sleep and defend each other in danger. The metaphor of the three-ply cord for strength in numbers is as old as the story of Gilgamesh (see Introduction).

The fourth "better" saying in chapter 4 opens a meditation on the fate of rulers (4:13-16). Wisdom is better than power; power does not make one person better than another. Verse 14 may reflect the stories of both people mentioned in verse 13. The poor but wise youth may come out of debtor's prison to reign. The foolish king may again become poor. In any case, the

Qoheleth

with the second youth who will succeed him. ¹⁶There is no end to all this people, to all who were before them; yet the later generations will not have joy in him. This also is vanity and a chase after wind.

Vanity of Many Words. ¹⁷Guard your step when you go to the house of God. Draw near for obedience, rather than for the fools' offering of sacrifice; for they know not how to keep from doing evil. 5 ¹Be not hasty in your utterance and let not your heart be quick to utter a promise in God's presence. God is in heaven and you are on earth; therefore let your words be few.

²As dreams come along with many cares,
so a fool's voice along with a multitude of words.

³When you make a vow to God, delay not its fulfillment. For God has no pleasure in fools; fulfill what you have vowed. ⁴It is better not to make a vow than make it and not fulfill it. ⁵Let not your utterances make you guilty, and say not before his representative, "It was a mistake." Why should God be angered by your words and destroy the works of your hands? ⁶Despite many dreams, futilities, and a multitude of words, fear God!

---

king will be succeeded by another (4:15), and later generations will neither remember nor rejoice in him (4:16).

4:17–5:6 Vanity of many words

Qoheleth turns to advice regarding one's relationship to God. With this section a common wisdom form begins to appear: admonitions ("do this," "don't do this"). The repetition of "dreams" and "a multitude of/multiply words" in 5:2 and 5:6 divides the section into two parts (4:17–5:2; 5:3-6).

The sage warns that people should watch their step in the temple (God's house). The purpose of worship is to listen to God's voice and obey, not to make a show of piety. Only the fool offers many sacrifices and then turns to evil. The verse is reminiscent of Samuel's warning to Saul: "Obedience is better than sacrifice" (1 Sam 15:22). The end of 4:17 can be interpreted sarcastically: "for they know not [or recognize not] how to keep from doing evil." The fool is too blind to recognize evil even in the doing of it. The fool also multiplies words (5:2). Jesus too warns against "babbling" in prayer (Matt 6:7-8). Thus to be wise is to be cautious and slow to speak in God's presence (5:1), aware of God's heavenly majesty. God is transcendent, totally beyond human imagination.

The warning about hasty speech becomes more specific in verses 3-5. The "vow" is a promise to take some action, for example, to offer a sacrifice; it does not refer to lifetime vows but to a temporary obligation. Qoheleth echoes Deuteronomy that it is better not to make a vow at all than to make it and not fulfill it (see Deut 23:22-24). One will be held guilty for failing to fulfill a vow. There is no excuse, no plea to God's representative that "it

Listen to God's word & obey.
Obedience is better than sacrifice

Gain and Loss of Goods. ⁷If you see oppression of the poor, and violation of rights and justice in the realm, do not be astonished by the fact, for the high official has another higher than he watching him and above these are others higher still—. ⁸But profitable for a land in such circumstances is a king concerned about cultivation.

⁹The covetous are never satisfied with money, nor lovers of wealth with their gain; so this too is vanity. ¹⁰Where there are great riches, there are also many to devour them. Of what use are they to the owner except as a feast for the eyes alone? ¹¹Sleep is sweet to the laborer, whether there is little or much to eat; but the abundance of the rich allows them no sleep.

¹²This is a grievous evil which I have seen under the sun: riches hoarded by their owners to their own hurt. ¹³Should the riches be lost through some misfortune, they may have offspring when they have no means. ¹⁴As they came forth from their mother's womb, so again shall they return, naked as they came, having nothing from their toil to bring with them. ¹⁵This too is a grievous evil, that they go just as they came. What then

---

was a mistake." The "representative" (literally "messenger") is surely the priest or some other minister in the sanctuary who is expecting the sacrificial offering. The word for "mistake" is used in the legal tradition for inadvertent failings (see Lev 4:2; 5:15; Num 15:22-31), but the making of a vow is not inadvertent. God will have no pleasure in an unfulfilled promise, even if the promise was made lightly; rather God's anger will be aroused. (It is also possible that the "utterance" in verse 5 is an oath taken lightly or another sin in speech; the consequence is the same.)

Verses 2 and 6 remind us of Qoheleth's observation that everything is fleeting. Dreams evaporate with the morning; many words are useless. The word translated "futilities" in verse 6 is the plural of *hebel*, the word translated "vanity" throughout the book. Only one thing is sure: fear God! The fear of the Lord is the awareness that God is God and I am not (5:1; see Ps 115:16). For human beings fear of the Lord is the only way to wisdom (see Job 28:28).

5:7-19 Gain and loss of goods

The next two sections (5:7-19; 6:1-9) parallel one another. The primary concern is possessions: problems with them and the enjoyment of them. Two verses (5:7-8), which are difficult to understand, introduce the sections. The idea is clear: Do not worry about what you cannot control; you cannot uproot all injustice. The reason is less clear. Either the bureaucracy is such that at every level there are officials "watching out" for each other, even if they practice injustice. Or people who are "high," the arrogant and ambitious, keep climbing (and trampling the "lowly"), even though there always

does it profit them to toil for the wind? ¹⁶All their days they eat in gloom with great vexation, sickness and resentment.

¹⁷Here is what I see as good: It is appropriate to eat and drink and prosper from all the toil one toils at under the sun during the limited days of life God gives us; for this is our lot. ¹⁸Those to whom God gives riches and property, and grants power to partake of them, so that they receive their lot and find joy in the fruits of their toil: This is a gift from God. ¹⁹For they will hardly dwell on the shortness of life, because God lets them busy themselves with the joy of their heart.

Limited Worth of Enjoyment. ¹There is another evil I have seen under the

---

seems to be another level above them. Verse 8 is more ambiguous. Does it mean that a king who cares about the state of agriculture is good for the land? Does such a king balance the upwardly mobile people in the previous verse? Is this a cryptic criticism of those who amass land without caring for its ongoing fertility? It is difficult to know.

The next two paragraphs (5:9-11, 12-16) portray problems with possessions: they never satisfy and they cannot be relied on. No matter what one has, it is not enough. Wealth also draws others who will "devour" it (5:10). These may be "hangers-on" who want to enjoy the wealth earned by others, for example, the newfound friends of the lottery winner! They may be the laborers upon whom the wealthy person depends for the increase of riches. In addition, worry about protecting wealth deprives the rich of sleep (5:11; see Sir 31:1-2). What good is wealth except to look at? All one needs is enough to eat and the sweetness of sleep.

A worse situation results from the sudden loss of riches when the hoarder has depended upon them (5:12-16). As Job says, "Naked I came forth from my mother's womb, / and naked shall I go back there" (Job 1:21). All human effort counts for nothing; there is not even anything to hand on to descendants. Why work so hard and deprive oneself of joy?

Qoheleth has only one solution: enjoy the gifts of God in the present moment (5:17-18). The final verse of the chapter may hold the most hope. There are two possible meanings. Either God gives joy so that human beings may be "preoccupied" with it and thus be distracted from the miseries and shortness of life. Or God "answers" human frailty with joy. In either case, joy is God's gift and happiness is found in the present moment.

6:1-9 Limited worth of enjoyment

At the beginning of chapter 6 the subjects of the previous section are repeated and reversed. Qoheleth advised the one to whom God gave "the power to partake" of riches to enjoy them (5:18). Now he acknowledges

sun, and it weighs heavily upon humankind: ²There is one to whom God gives riches and property and honor, and who lacks nothing the heart could desire; yet God does not grant the power to partake of them, but a stranger devours them. This is vanity and a dire plague. ³Should one have a hundred children and live many years, no matter to what great age, still if one has not the full benefit of those goods, I proclaim that the child born dead, even if left unburied, is more fortunate. ⁴Though it came in vain and goes into darkness and its name is enveloped in darkness, ⁵though it has not seen the sun or known anything, yet the dead child has more peace. ⁶Should such a one live twice a thousand years and not enjoy those goods, do not both go to the same place?

⁷All human toil is for the mouth, yet the appetite is never satisfied. ⁸What profit have the wise compared to fools, or what profit have the lowly in knowing how to conduct themselves in life? ⁹"What the eyes see is better than what the desires wander after." This also is vanity and a chase after wind.

---

that sometimes this does not work. There may be someone to whom God grants riches but not "the power to partake" of them (6:2). The wealth is not even passed down to descendants (see 2:18-21) but goes to a "stranger," someone outside the family. This is in contrast to the one who has lost wealth and has nothing to hand down to descendants (5:13).

The next four verses (6:3-6) are bound off by exaggerated numbers: a hundred children, a lifetime of two thousand years. Just as great riches do not satisfy (5:9-10), neither do many children and many years of life (6:3). The common blessings of wisdom were understood to be wealth, old age, and descendants (see Job 42:16; Prov 8:18; Ps 112:2-3). These things provided a kind of pseudo-immortality, but Psalm 49 points out that everyone must die. Two thousand years (6:6) is twice the age of Methuselah (Gen 5:27)! But even that is not enough. If one does not enjoy one's goods, that is, if one does not enjoy the present moment, then all is worthless. The child born dead, the most hopeless example of mortality, is more fortunate, because the child does not know what it has missed (6:4-5). In the end, Qoheleth believes, everyone dies and goes to Sheol (6:6; see Introduction).

The goal of all human desire is life, beginning with food, but no one is ever fully satisfied (6:7). So the wise, whether rich or poor, have no advantage (6:8). Qoheleth quotes a proverb meaning that it is better to focus on the reality that is seen than what is only wished for. But even the proverb is vanity (6:9)! This is the last appearance of the phrase: "vanity and a chase after wind."

Live in the present . . . moment

II. Qoheleth's Conclusions

¹⁰Whatever is, was long ago given its name, and human nature is known; mortals cannot contend in judgment with One who is stronger. ¹¹For the more words, the more vanity; what profit is there for anyone? ¹²For who knows what is good for mortals in life, the limited days of their vain life, spent like a shadow? Because who can tell them what will come afterward under the sun?

A. No One Can Find Out the Best Way of Acting

Critique of Sages on the Day of Adversity

7 ¹A good name is better than good ointment,
and the day of death than the day of birth.
²It is better to go to the house of mourning
than to the house of feasting,

QOHELETH'S CONCLUSIONS

Ecclesiastes 6:10–11:6

The second half of the book is introduced in 6:10-12. The ideas have appeared before. What exists was created, that is, "called by name," long ago (see 1:9-10; 3:15). Human nature—the Hebrew word is *adam*—is known to be earthly (from the *adamah*, the earth) and mortal. Humans cannot contend with God (the one who is stronger), although there are several examples of those who have tried (see Job 9:3; 23:6; Jer 12:1). Human words are empty; in verse 11 the words themselves sound like babbling: *yesh-debarim harebbeh marbim habel*. Verse 12 introduces a key idea of the second half: "who knows?" Who knows what is good for mortals? Who knows what the future will bring? Human life vanishes like a shadow.

7:1-14 Critique of sages on the day of adversity

This is the first of three collections of proverbs in the book (see 9:17–10:4; 10:8–11:4). The key to interpreting this section lies in the characteristic ambiguity of the proverb in general and the juxtaposition of proverbs here. Proverbs are by nature ambiguous. The meaning of any proverb is shaped by the context. It takes wisdom to interpret and use a proverb, as is shown by the juxtaposition of two seemingly contradictory proverbs in the book of Proverbs (26:4-5). To take a modern example: Is it better to consider all the alternatives before acting ("Look before you leap") or to act immediately ("He who hesitates is lost")? Qoheleth capitalizes on this paradoxical character of proverbs. He seems to be responding to his own question: "who knows what is good?" (6:12). The word "good/better" (*tob*) occurs eleven times in these fourteen verses.

For that is the end of every mortal,
and the living should take it to
heart.
³Sorrow is better than laughter;
when the face is sad, the heart
grows wise.
⁴The heart of the wise is in the
house of mourning,
but the heart of fools is in the
house of merriment.
⁵It is better to listen to the rebuke of
the wise
than to listen to the song of
fools;
⁶For as the crackling of thorns
under a pot,
so is the fool's laughter.
This also is vanity.

⁷Extortion can make a fool out of
the wise,
and a bribe corrupts the heart.
⁸Better is the end of a thing than its
beginning;
better is a patient spirit than a
lofty one.
⁹Do not let anger upset your spirit,
for anger lodges in the bosom of
a fool.

¹⁰Do not say: How is it that former times were better than these? For it is not out of wisdom that you ask about this.

¹¹Wisdom is as good as an
inheritance
and profitable to those who see
the sun.

The topic in verses 1-4 might well be St. Benedict's advice: "Keep death daily before your eyes" (RB 4.47). Verse 1 begins with a common idea: reputation is better than wealth and pleasure. The proverb is enhanced by its sound: *tob shem misshemen tob* (see commentary on Song 1:3). But the second half of the verse seems to subvert the first half. Why is the day of death better? Because a good name, a good reputation, is only certain at death. Before death it is possible to lose one's reputation. The opening proverb is simply carried to its logical conclusion. Therefore it is better to go to a funeral than a wedding in order to remember that death comes to everyone. Sorrow, acknowledging the whole reality of human life, is better than shallow merrymaking. Literally, by a bad/sad face the heart is made good (or glad or wise). Honesty in facing death distinguishes the wise and the foolish.

The contrast between the wise and the foolish is continued in verses 5-7. Heeding a wise rebuke leads to wisdom (Prov 13:1; 17:10). The fool's song may be empty praise. The Hebrew word for "song" (*shir*) leads to the image in verse 6: the crackling of thorns (*sirim*) under a pot (*sir*). Thorns used for fuel produce more sound than heat; the fool's noisy laughter and song do not produce wisdom. Qoheleth says, however, that even here is vanity. Why? Even the wise can be made foolish by too much stress, whether the distress of extortion or the potential pleasure of a bribe (7:7).

Verses 8-10 return to the question of the "better" time that was introduced in verse 1. The end is better than the beginning just as the day of death is

¹²For the protection of wisdom is as the protection of money; and knowledge is profitable because wisdom gives life to those who possess it.

¹³Consider the work of God. Who can make straight what God has made crooked? ¹⁴On a good day enjoy good things, and on an evil day consider: Both the one and the other God has made, so that no one may find the least fault with him.

Critique of Sages on Justice and Wickedness. ¹⁵I have seen all manner of things in my vain days: the just perishing in their justice, and the wicked living long in their wickedness. ¹⁶"Be not just to excess, and be not overwise. Why work your own ruin? ¹⁷Be not wicked to excess, and be not foolish. Why should you die before your time?" ¹⁸It is good to hold to this rule, and not to let that one go; but the one who fears God will succeed with both.

---

better than the day of birth. Thus it is better to have the ability to wait, to have a "long spirit" (NABRE: "patient spirit") than to have a "high spirit" (NABRE: "lofty" spirit) arrogantly assuming at the beginning that something will come to a successful conclusion (7:8). Even this truth, however, is not absolute. Although one must not be too hastily upset by anger, neither must one be a fool and nurse anger patiently in one's heart (see Sir 27:30). Nor can one say that the past was a "better" time. One of Qoheleth's primary messages is that the best time to live is the present (see 3:11-13; 9:7).

In verses 11-14 Qoheleth concludes that wisdom is profitable, but he does not repeat the common tradition that wisdom is "better" than gold and silver (see Prov 3:14; 8:19). It is only *as good as* an inheritance. Verse 12 is ambiguous, as the Hebrew reads literally: "in the shadow of wisdom, in the shadow of money." Is wisdom a shelter, a protection, just as money can shelter one from some of the difficulties of life? Or is wisdom, like money, as fleeting as a shadow? The NABRE has opted for the former. In any case, the sage considers wisdom profitable because it enables one to live.

The bottom line in this collection of proverbs is that human beings cannot really know what is good because they can neither understand nor change the works of God (7:13-14). Qoheleth sees God as the source for both good and evil (see 1 Sam 2:6-7; Job 2:10), but in no way can human beings contend with God (see 6:10).

7:15-25 Critique of sages on justice and wickedness

Qoheleth now grounds his advice in experience. He has seen both good and bad, all manner of things. Worst of all he has realized that righteousness does not guarantee long life, nor do the wicked always die young. This contradicts traditional wisdom (see Prov 11:4-7) and prompts the advice to avoid extremes of righteousness and wisdom (7:16). The sage is not against striving to be righteous; he is against the presumption that one

¹⁹Wisdom is a better defense for the wise than ten princes in the city, ²⁰yet there is no one on earth so just as to do good and never sin. ²¹Do not give your heart to every word that is spoken; you may hear your servant cursing you, ²²for your heart knows that you have many times cursed others.

²³All these things I probed in wisdom. I said, "I will acquire wisdom"; but it was far beyond me. ²⁴What exists is far-reaching; it is deep, very deep: Who can find it out? ²⁵I turned my heart toward knowledge; I sought and pursued wisdom and its design, and I recognized that wickedness is foolishness and folly is madness.

Critique of Advice on Women. ²⁶More bitter than death I find the woman who is a hunter's trap, whose heart is a snare, whose hands are prison bonds. The one who pleases God will be delivered from her, but the one who displeases will be entrapped by her. ²⁷See, this have I found, says Qoheleth, adding one to one to find the sum. ²⁸What my soul still seeks and has yet to find is this: "One man out of a thousand have I found, but

can be perfectly and completely righteous by one's own effort. He is also against the presumption that the possession of wisdom in its fullness is available to human beings. Such presumption and perfectionism will inevitably lead to psychological and physical disaster. On the other hand, one must not simply give up and go to the extremes of wickedness and folly (7:17). That too leads to death. Rather one must strive for good while recognizing one's own weakness. The fear of God, that is, the recognition of God's infinite power and one's own finite frailty, is the way to live well (7:18). There is true wisdom.

Verses 19-25 demonstrate the limitations of righteousness and wisdom. The inevitability of sin shows one's flaws (7:20). Awareness of others' weaknesses in speech reveals one's own similar faults (7:21-22). Try as he might, Qoheleth cannot attain the perfection of wisdom (7:23). Another characteristic question of this second half of the book appears here: Who can find out?

7:26-29 Critique of advice on women

These verses are the most difficult to interpret in the book and they have been the cause of much persecution of women. Qoheleth has declared his intention to seek wisdom and its design (7:25). In this section he continues his search (7:27-28). He begins, however, with a warning against "the woman" who is a trap (7:26). The warning may simply be an echo of the proverbial advice against adultery (Prov 2:16-19; 5:1-14; 6:20–7:27). In the context of the search for wisdom, however, this woman may be the personification of Folly, mentioned in verse 25, whose guests end up in Sheol (Prov 9:13-18). Wisdom, on the other hand, is the valiant woman: Who can

a woman among them all I have not found." [29]But this alone I have found: God made humankind honest, but they have pursued many designs.

Critique of Advice to Heed Authority

8 [1]Who is like the wise person,
  and who knows the explanation
    of things?
Wisdom illumines the face
  and transforms a grim
    countenance.

[2]Observe the command of the king, in view of your oath to God. [3]Be not hasty to withdraw from the king; do not persist in an unpleasant situation, for he does whatever he pleases. [4]His word is sovereign, and who can say to him, "What are you doing?"

[5]"Whoever observes a command knows no harm, and the wise heart knows times and judgments." [6]Yes, there is a time and a judgment for everything. But it is a great evil for mortals [7]that they are ignorant of what is to come; for who will make known to them how it will be? [8]No one is master of the breath of life so as to retain it, and none has mastery of the day of death. There is no exemption in wartime, nor does wickedness deliver those who practice it. [9]All these things I saw and I applied my heart to every

find her (Prov 31:10; see Eccl 7:24)? The word "find" occurs seven times in this passage, the word "seek" three times.

Qoheleth has recognized the web of wickedness, folly, and madness (7:25). He still seeks the design, the answer. He has *not* found the proverb true that there is one [good] man in a thousand but no woman (7:28). ("I still seek and have yet to find.") He has found only this, that God made all humankind (*adam*) honest, but they have pursued many (devious?) designs (7:29).

This interpretation, adopted by the NABRE, softens but does not remove Qoheleth's misogynism. Other scholars consider verse 28b to be a later insertion in the chapter. The passage remains mysterious, open to many interpretations. All interpreters seek and have yet to find!

8:1-9 Critique of advice to heed authority

The previous chapter ended with Qoheleth still seeking wisdom and its design. Now he exclaims: Who knows! That statement about the search for wisdom in general leads to practical advice on how to behave in the presence of the king. Such advice is common in Proverbs (e.g., Prov 16:12-15). First of all, it is wise to look pleasant in the presence of authority (8:1). Usually it is God who illumines the face (Num 6:25; Pss 67:2; 80:4); here it is wisdom, and perhaps the practical wisdom of necessity. Respect for the authority of the king is demanded (8:2). Two phrases that describe his authority are otherwise used of God (8:3-4): "he does whatever he pleases" (see Ps 135:6) and "who can say to him, 'What are you doing?'" (see Job

work that is done under the sun, while one person tyrannizes over another for harm.

The Problem of Retribution. [10]Meanwhile I saw the wicked buried. They would come and go from the holy place. But those were forgotten in the city who had acted justly. This also is vanity. [11]Because the sentence against an evil deed is not promptly executed, the human heart is filled with the desire to commit evil— [12]because the sinner does evil a hundred times and survives. Though indeed I know that it shall be well with those who fear God, for their reverence toward him; [13]and that it shall not be well with the wicked, who shall not prolong their shadowy days, for their lack of reverence toward God.

[14]This is a vanity that occurs on earth: There are those who are just but are treated as though they had done evil, and those who are wicked but are treated as though they had done justly. This, too, I say is vanity. [15]Therefore I praised joy, because there is nothing better for mortals under the sun than to eat and to drink and to be joyful; this will accompany them in their toil through the limited days of life God gives them under the sun.

[16]I applied my heart to know wisdom and to see the business that is done on

---

9:12; Isa 45:9). The wise person considers when to stay with the king and when to yield (8:3). Verse 5 seems to summarize the wisdom of the previous verses: obedience and knowledge of times.

But Qoheleth has said previously that humans do not know the appropriate times (see 3:11). They do not know the future (8:6-7). They cannot even control the extent of their lives (8:8). Even if it is possible to be exempt from war (see Deut 20:5-8) or to pay someone to substitute in the military draft as was done in the Persian period, no one can escape the final battle of death. Humans, who do not have power over breath or death, however, do have power to tyrannize one another (8:9). The sage continues to observe and ponder.

8:10-17 The problem of retribution

The violent injustice which ends verse 9 leads to a reflection on another injustice: the wicked are honored in burial and remembered for frequent visits to the temple while the just are forgotten (8:10). The wicked, who by rights should suffer for their wrongdoing, seem to prosper, and this inequity leads others into wrongdoing (8:11-12). It is the problem of Psalm 73: "I was envious of the arrogant / when I saw the prosperity of the wicked. / For they suffer no pain; / their bodies are healthy and sleek" (Ps 73:3-4). Qoheleth comes to the same conclusion as the psalmist. This injustice will not last (8:12-13). God sets the wicked "on a slippery road" and "suddenly they are devastated" (Ps 73:18-19). But good will come to the just. The distinguishing mark is again fear of the Lord.

earth, though neither by day nor by night do one's eyes see sleep, [17]and I saw all the work of God: No mortal can find out the work that is done under the sun. However much mortals may toil in searching, no one finds it out; and even if the wise claim to know, they are unable to find it out.

B. No One Knows the Future

9 [1]All this I have kept in my heart and all this I examined: The just, the wise, and their deeds are in the hand of God. Love from hatred mortals cannot tell; both are before them. [2]Everything is the same for everybody: the same lot for the just and the wicked, for the good, for the clean and the unclean, for the one who offers sacrifice and the one who does not. As it is for the good, so it is for the sinner; as it is for the one who takes an oath, so it is for the one who fears an oath. [3]Among all the things that are done under the sun, this is the worst, that there is one lot for all. Hence the hearts of human beings are filled with evil, and madness is in their hearts during life; and afterward—to the dead!

[4]For whoever is chosen among all the living has hope: "A live dog is better off than a dead lion." [5]For the living know that they are to die, but the dead no longer know anything. There is no further recompense for them, because all memory of them is lost. [6]For them, love and hatred and rivalry have long since perished. Never again will they have part in anything that is done under the sun.

[7]Go, eat your bread with joy and drink your wine with a merry heart, be-

After his declaration of faith that God will eventually make things right, Qoheleth returns to the problem that the wicked prosper and the just suffer. His solution is familiar: cultivate joy in the present moment (8:14-15).

The sage continues to search for wisdom, aware that no one can understand the work of God. The refrain, "find out," is repeated three times in verse 17.

9:1-10 Live in the present

Qoheleth redefines his problem: the commonness of common human experience! "Everything is the same for everybody." Mortals cannot understand the actions of God, whether apparently favorable (love) or unfavorable (hate). Yet no one can escape the hand of God. No matter how people distinguish themselves from one another, everyone dies. Still the sage affirms the goodness of life (9:4-6). Even a dog, a despised animal, is better off when alive than the great lion that is dead. Qoheleth's understanding of the place of the dead, Sheol, is clear: the dead know nothing; they forget and are forgotten; they no longer have any relationship with anyone; they no longer have any purposeful activity. So Qoheleth returns to his advice to enjoy life now (9:7-9). The present moment is all anyone has. Take full advantage of whatever the moment brings.

cause it is now that God favors your works. ⁸At all times let your garments be white, and spare not the perfume for your head. ⁹Enjoy life with the wife you love, all the days of the vain life granted you under the sun. This is your lot in life, for the toil of your labors under the sun. ¹⁰Anything you can turn your hand to, do with what power you have; for there will be no work, no planning, no knowledge, no wisdom in Sheol where you are going.

The Time of Misfortune Is Not Known. ¹¹Again I saw under the sun that the race is not won by the swift, nor the battle by the valiant, nor a livelihood by the wise, nor riches by the shrewd, nor favor by the experts; for a time of misfortune comes to all alike. ¹²Human beings no more know their own time than fish taken in the fatal net or birds trapped in the snare; like these, mortals are caught when an evil time suddenly falls upon them.

The Uncertain Future and the Sages. ¹³On the other hand I saw this wise deed under the sun, which I thought magnificent. ¹⁴Against a small city with few inhabitants advanced a mighty king, who surrounded it and threw up great siegeworks about it. ¹⁵But in the city lived a man who, though poor, was wise, and he delivered it through his wisdom. Yet no one remembered this poor man. ¹⁶Though I had said, "Wisdom is better than force," yet the wisdom of the poor man is despised and his words go unheeded.

> ¹⁷The quiet words of the wise are better heeded
> than the shout of a ruler of fools.
> ¹⁸Wisdom is better than weapons of war,
> but one bungler destroys much good.

10 ¹Dead flies corrupt and spoil the perfumer's oil;
> more weighty than wisdom or wealth is a little folly!
> ²The wise heart turns to the right;
> the foolish heart to the left.

9:11-12 The time of misfortune is not known

The question of the appropriate time returns (see 3:1-15). It is impossible to predict by human wisdom who will succeed and who will fail. It is as impossible for human beings to know what will happen in the future as it is for any animal.

9:13–10:14 The uncertain future and the sages

This section consists of an example story (9:13-18) and several loosely connected sayings. First Qoheleth turns to a story to illustrate a point: the wisdom of a poor man is more powerful than the siege works of a mighty king. However, the people saved by the poor man forget him, presumably because of his lower social status. It is a story of little and great: a great example ("magnificent," 9:13); a "small city" (9:14); a "mighty king" who "threw up great siegeworks" (9:14). It is also a story of misplaced priorities: the inhabitants of the city value wealth above wisdom. Two proverbial

³Even when walking in the street the fool, lacking understanding, calls everyone a fool.

⁴Should the anger of a ruler burst upon you, do not yield your place; for calmness abates great offenses.

⁵I have seen under the sun another evil, like a mistake that proceeds from a tyrant: ⁶a fool put in high position, while the great and the rich sit in lowly places. ⁷I have seen slaves on horseback, while princes went on foot like slaves.

⁸Whoever digs a pit may fall into it,
and whoever breaks through a
wall, a snake may bite.

⁹Whoever quarries stones may be
hurt by them,
and whoever chops wood is in
danger from it.

¹⁰If the ax becomes dull, and the blade is not sharpened, then effort must be increased. But the advantage of wisdom is success.

¹¹If the snake bites before it is
charmed,
then there is no advantage in a
charmer.
¹²Words from the mouth of the wise
win favor,
but the lips of fools consume
them.

---

sayings lay bare the contradiction (9:17-18). What is "better" can be destroyed by just one "bungler."

The theme that it takes very little to destroy great good is continued in chapter 10. Just one or two dead flies may cause the perfumer's oil to ferment and possibly change the odor. Just a little folly can pervert wisdom (10:1). This observation leads to a meditation on folly. In biblical times the heart was understood to be the seat of intelligence and will. One thought and acted from the heart. The hearts of the wise and foolish go in opposite directions. The "right" is the direction of goodness and favor; the "left" is the direction of ignorance and disaster. (Compare "sinister" or "gauche" in English, both of which mean "left.") Fools, turning to the left, lack "heart" (i.e., understanding). Thus they either call everyone else a fool or announce (by their actions?) that they themselves are fools (10:3).

The subject of conduct in the presence of a powerful person returns (10:4; see 8:2-4). This ruler is not a king but probably some high official. In contrast to 8:3, the advice here is to remain steadfast even in the face of anger. The attitude, however, seems to be similar: remain calm. The saying echoes a proverb: "By patience is a ruler persuaded, / and a soft tongue can break a bone" (Prov 25:15).

The anger of the previous ruler suggests the folly of another powerful person, a tyrant (10:5). His "mistake" (the word suggests an inadvertent error) turns the world upside down (10:6-7). Fools have replaced official advisors; commoners have replaced the elite. The horses upon which slaves

¹³The beginning of their words is
folly,
and the end of their talk is utter
madness;
¹⁴yet fools multiply words.
No one knows what is to come,
for who can tell anyone what
will be?
¹⁵The toil of fools wearies them,
so they do not know even the
way to town.

No One Knows What Evil Will Come

¹⁶Woe to you, O land, whose king is
a youth,
and whose princes feast in the
morning!

¹⁷Happy are you, O land, whose
king is of noble birth,
and whose princes dine at the
right time—
for vigor and not in drinking
bouts.
¹⁸Because of laziness, the rafters sag;
when hands are slack, the house
leaks.
¹⁹A feast is made for merriment
and wine gives joy to the living,
but money answers for everything.
²⁰Even in your thoughts do not
curse the king,
nor in the privacy of your
bedroom curse the rich;

---

are riding are a sign of wealth and power. Horses are not native to Israel; few could afford them. They are ordinarily used for military purposes or as regal transport. Ordinary people rode donkeys or walked. The stability of the social order is a value in the wisdom tradition.

Life is risky for everyone; the laborer faces danger also (10:8-9). The hunter digs a pit for an animal to fall into and camouflages it. But if he is careless and his camouflage works too well, he falls into it himself. The walls between fields and of houses were built of stones with smaller stones used as mortar, a perfect place for snakes to hide. The worker who takes down a wall risks a poisonous bite. Anyone who uses sharp tools is also in danger, both from the tools and from the material worked by them.

Practical wisdom teaches ways to diminish the risk (10:10). Sharpen the tools; charm the snake. The charmer is called the "master of the tongue," the master of languages even of snakes. There is advantage in wisdom, but sometimes even wisdom does not help (10:11). Sometimes danger comes unexpectedly or is more powerful than human prevention.

This last collection of sayings (10:12-15) is held together by the words "fool" and "fool" (compare 9:17–10:3). The subject is a favorite wisdom topic: speech. There is only one comment about the wise: the words of the wise win favor (but see 9:11). The sage's attention is on the babbling of fools. From beginning to end their words are folly, yet they cannot stop. They more than anyone do not know what is going to happen, yet they keep

> For the birds of the air may carry
> your voice,
> a winged creature may tell what
> you say.
>
> 11 ¹Send forth your bread upon the
> face of the waters;
>
> after a long time you may find it
> again.
> ²Make seven, or even eight
> portions;
> you know not what misfortune
> may come upon the earth.

talking. They do not even know the way to town, a sign of absolute incompetence! The section ends with this repetition of "do not know."

10:16–11:2 No one knows what evil will come

Several sayings are gathered in this unit, bound off by the repetition in 11:2 of "not know." Verses 16-17 proclaim a woe and a beatitude concerning the character of leaders in a land. The word translated "youth" can also mean "servant." (This compares to the derogatory use of "boy" in English.) So the ruler in verse 16 may be immature or may belong to a lower class (see 10:6-7). His princes dissipate their strength by feasting and carousing in the morning, thus by implication all day. The contrast is a mature and well-born king whose princes know the proper time (see 8:5) and have good judgment. They too feast, but as strong men who have self-control.

The simple meaning of the proverbs in verses 18-19 is obvious: laziness brings disaster; feasting brings joy; money answers for everything! These are all themes that recur in traditional wisdom, although there are often warnings about money (Prov 11:4; 13:11). The joy in feasting is particularly important to Qoheleth (see 8:15; 9:7). It is also possible, however, to read these proverbs in the context of the previous verses. If the leaders of a land are dissolute and lazy (see 10:16), the "house," that is, the kingdom or the dynasty, may collapse. Perhaps such leaders, whose wealth makes them callous to the needs of others, focus only on feasting.

Verse 20 returns to the subject of rulers; the topic, however, is caution in criticism. The image of birds carrying one's voice is common in the ancient Near Eastern wisdom tradition and in the modern English proverb: "A little bird told me." In this context the proverb may be a warning to those who live in the land described in 10:16!

There is serious disagreement concerning the interpretation of 11:1-2. The traditional interpretation, both in Jewish and Christian tradition, is that one is advised to be generous. A good gift today may be rewarded in the future; give generously to many people, even if the future looks bleak. It is also possible to interpret the verses as economic advice: Send out your goods, you may get a return on your investment (hopefully also a profit). Diversify your investments as a protection against disaster. Finally, Qoheleth

No One Knows What Good Will Come

³When the clouds are full,
they pour out rain upon the earth.
Whether a tree falls to the south or
to the north,
wherever it falls, there shall it lie.
⁴One who pays heed to the wind
will never sow,
and one who watches the clouds
will never reap.
⁵Just as you do not know how the
life breath
enters the human frame in the
mother's womb,
So you do not know the work of
God,
who is working in everything.
⁶In the morning sow your seed,
and at evening do not let your
hand be idle:
For you do not know which of the
two will be successful,
or whether both alike will turn
out well.

Poem on Youth and Old Age. ⁷Light is sweet! and it is pleasant for the eyes to see the sun. ⁸However many years mortals may live, let them, as they enjoy them all, remember that the days of darkness will be many. All that is to come is vanity.

⁹Rejoice, O youth, while you are
young
and let your heart be glad in the
days of your youth.
Follow the ways of your heart,
the vision of your eyes;
Yet understand regarding all this
that God will bring you to
judgment.

---

may typically be commenting on the phrase, "you don't know." Do something that seems foolish. It may turn out well; it may not! In any case, these verses illustrate the rich ambiguity of proverbs!

11:3-6 No one knows what good will come

The final verses in this section emphasize human ignorance. Especially among farmers there are certain folk sayings about the weather that are frequently recited, but the most common wisdom is that no one can control the weather. Anyone who waits for the perfect conditions will never act. What human beings think they know is never certain. The comments on the weather lead to a meditation on a greater mystery: the coming of new life in the womb (11:5; see Ps 139:14-16). The repetition of words links the two subjects: "wind/breath" (Hebrew *ruah*) in verses 4-5; "full" and "the full one" (i.e., the pregnant one) in verses 3 and 5. "Wind/breath" has appeared several times. The wind constantly shifts (1:6). Human effort is "a chase after wind" (1:14, 17; etc.). Is the life-breath of humans and beasts the same (3:19, 21)? No one can master the breath of life (8:8). The mystery of breath and wind leads to Qoheleth's main point in this section: Mortals do not know the work of God (see 3:11; 7:13; 8:17). What is to be done? Act wisely; work regularly. Qoheleth implies but never says this: Trust God. The threefold repetition of "you do not know" closes this section (11:5-6).

¹⁰Banish misery from your heart
and remove pain from your
body,
for youth and black hair are
fleeting.

◄ **12** ¹Remember your Creator in the
days of your youth,
before the evil days come
And the years approach of which
you will say,
"I have no pleasure in them";
²Before the sun is darkened
and the light and the moon and
the stars
and the clouds return after the
rain;
³When the guardians of the house
tremble,
and the strong men are bent;
When the women who grind are
idle because they are few,
and those who look through the
windows grow blind;
⁴When the doors to the street are
shut,
and the sound of the mill is low;
When one rises at the call of a bird,
and all the daughters of song
are quiet;

POEM ON YOUTH AND OLD AGE

Ecclesiastes 11:7–12:8

The book opened with the cycles of nature that seemed endless; it closes with everything coming to an end. The final poem can be considered in two parts (11:7-10; 12:1-7). The first part is Qoheleth's final advice to enjoy life. It is addressed to a youth, a young man in full vigor. Two imperatives characterize the section: remember and rejoice. Remember that the "days of darkness," that is, old age and death, are coming; rejoice in the days of your youth (11:7-8). The rejoicing requires positive and negative actions (11:10): Remove pain from your heart and body; follow your heart and eyes. The comment concerning God's judgment seems out of place (11:9). Throughout the book, however, Qoheleth has advised the reader to fear God and to remember God's judgment (see 3:17; 5:6; 6:10; 8:12). Enjoyment of the present moment is God's gift (see 3:13; 5:18; 8:15). God judges whether one has taken full advantage of what has been given.

The second part of the poem (12:1-8) opens with the key word "remember." The spelling of the next word in Hebrew leads to two interpretations: "Remember your Creator" can also be read "remember your grave." Qoheleth keeps the focus on the beginning and the end. The remaining verses have several layers of meaning. It is generally agreed that they have to do with old age and death. They may be read, at least in part, as an allegory of old age. In this reading the women who grind are the teeth; those who look through the window are the eyes; the guardians of the house are the limbs, and so on. Parts of the poem seem to be simple descriptions of aging: fear of heights, gray hair (the white almond blossoms), the failure of stimu-

⁵When one is afraid of heights,
and perils in the street;
When the almond tree blooms,
and the locust grows sluggish
and the caper berry is without
effect,
Because mortals go to their lasting
home,
and mourners go about the
streets;
⁶Before the silver cord is snapped
and the golden bowl is broken,
And the pitcher is shattered at the
spring,
and the pulley is broken at the
well,

⁷And the dust returns to the earth
as it once was,
and the life breath returns to
God who gave it.
⁸Vanity of vanities, says Qoheleth,
all things are vanity!

Epilogue. ⁹Besides being wise, Qoheleth taught the people knowledge, and weighed, scrutinized and arranged many proverbs. ¹⁰Qoheleth sought to find appropriate sayings, and to write down true sayings with precision. ¹¹The sayings of the wise are like goads; like fixed spikes are the collected sayings given by one shepherd. ¹²As to more than

lants to rouse the appetite (caper berry). Second, the poem may be read as a description not only of the old age and death of one person but as the eschatological end of the world. The light of sun and moon and stars is darkened (see Matt 24:29). Even strong men tremble and bow down. "Two women will be grinding at the mill; one will be taken, and one will be left" (Matt 24:41). The human being (*adam*) goes to his lasting home. Third, there are suggestions of the funeral rite and death. Mourners are in the street. Pottery is shattered; broken pottery is often found in graves in the ancient Near East, a symbol that the human being, an earthen vessel, has been destroyed. The flesh returns to dust and the breath returns to God. Verse 7 does not reflect the Greek notion of body and soul; rather it indicates that at death there is no longer a living human person: the parts (dust and breath) have each returned to their source. The destruction of the lamp (the silver cord and golden bowl) and of vessels for water is also symbolic of death (12:6). There is no need to impose a single grid of interpretation. The poem is powerful precisely because all these layers of meaning are suggested.

Qoheleth's work concludes with a repetition of the opening statement: all things are vanity (12:8; see 1:2).

EPILOGUE

Ecclesiastes 12:9-14

An editor added these comments about Qoheleth and his book. Qoheleth is praised for his work and his wisdom, but there is a warning against an

these, my son, beware. Of the making of many books there is no end, and in much study there is weariness for the flesh.

[13]The last word, when all is heard: Fear God and keep his commandments, for this concerns all humankind; [14]because God will bring to judgment every work, with all its hidden qualities, whether good or bad.

---

excess of searching for more wisdom or more books. The summary of Qoheleth's message is simple: Fear God and keep the commandments. Keeping the commandments is not clearly mentioned by Qoheleth in the body of the book, but it is a natural corollary to the fear of God (see Deut 5:29; 8:6). This comment too is followed by a warning about God's judgment (12:14).

Esther

The book of Esther tells the story of a Jewish woman and her uncle who, by their courage and wit, deliver the Jews from threatened genocide. The drama and humor of the story, which is characterized by exaggeration and irony, is appreciated best when the book is read aloud. Esther, one of the Megilloth ("scrolls"; see Introduction to the Festival Scrolls), is known in Jewish tradition as the Megillah, *the* Scroll.

Versions and canonicity

The book of Esther has come to us in Hebrew and Greek versions. The Greek version is a free translation of the Hebrew but with some significant differences. The major difference is found in the six additions, lettered A–F in the NABRE. In the Hebrew version, probably closest to the original, God is never mentioned, nor is the covenant or the observance of the law or customs regarding diet and marriage. The primary festivals—Passover, Pentecost, and Booths—are missing; the only festival that appears is Purim. The silence about faith is remedied in the Greek version: God is mentioned by name or title over fifty times (in the additions but also in the main text); addition C presents the prayers of Mordecai and Esther, and Esther bemoans her marriage to a Gentile. Addition D heightens the drama as Esther risks her life for her people. Additions B and E are supposed copies of official decrees. Additions A and F set an apocalyptic tone with the description of a dream and its interpretation. The reader will discover that the story has a different emphasis in the two versions. In the Hebrew version Esther and Mordecai are the heroes; in the Greek version God is the hero. In the Hebrew version the focus is on the deliverance of the Jews and the establishment of Purim; in the Greek version the focus is on God's work through Esther.

The Hebrew version is accepted as canonical in the Jewish and Protestant traditions; the Greek version is canonical in the Roman Catholic and Orthodox traditions. The NABRE translation represents the Hebrew version with the Greek additions.

History or fiction

The background of the story is the reign of the Persian king Xerxes the Great (485–465 B.C.). The representation of fifth-century Persia and the court seems to be accurate, judging by the descriptions of the contemporary Greek historian Herodotus. Details such as court customs, the efficient postal system, the winter court at Susa, as well as several Persian loan words in the text, give a sense of historicity to the book. Other elements, however, indicate the fictional character of the story: Persian kings could choose queens from only seven noble families and Xerxes' queen was named Amestris. The official language of Persia was Aramaic, and it is unlikely that decrees would be sent out in "all languages." Exaggerations such as the six-month feast and the over-reaction to Vashti's refusal also show the work of a master storyteller, as do ironic details such as Haman's execution on the very scaffold he prepared for Mordecai.

Structure

The book is carefully structured. The dream (add. A) is balanced by its interpretation (add. F). The banquets of the king and queen in chapter 1 are balanced by Esther's two banquets in chapters 5 and 7. The decree authorizing the annihilation of the Jews (ch. 3 and add. B) is balanced by the decree authorizing the Jews to kill their enemies (ch. 8 and add. E). The prayers of Mordecai and Esther and Esther's approach to the king are at the center of the book (adds. C–D).

Purim

The establishment of the festival of Purim as the celebration of deliverance is described in 9:20-32. The name is derived from the Babylonian word for "lot," *puru*. Its observance is characterized by feasting and gift giving. The story of Esther is told (and dramatized) with much cheering and jeering. The Talmud suggests drinking to the point that one can no longer distinguish between "Blessed be Mordecai" and "Cursed be Haman." The secular nature of the celebration may indicate its non-Jewish origins, possibly a festival marking the Persian New Year.

Esther

I. Prologue

A Dream of Mordecai. ¹In the second year of the reign of Ahasuerus the great, on the first day of Nisan, Mordecai, son of Jair, son of Shimei, son of Kish, of the tribe of Benjamin, had a dream. ²He was a Jew residing in the city of Susa, a prominent man who served at the king's court, ³and one of the captives whom Nebuchadnezzar, king of Babylon, had taken from Jerusalem with Jeconiah, king of Judah.

⁴This was his dream. There was noise and tumult, thunder and earthquake—confusion upon the earth. ⁵Two great

PROLOGUE

Esther A:1-17

A:1-11 Dream of Mordecai

The story of Esther begins with a prelude, the first of the Greek additions. (Much of the material here, with some differences, is also found in 2:5-6, 19-23 of the Hebrew version.) In the NABRE the name of the king (see Introduction) has been rendered throughout as "Ahasuerus," although in the Greek additions he is called "Artaxerxes." The first paragraph sets the stage. The time is the second regnal year of Ahasuerus, thus a year before the events of the first chapter of the Hebrew story (see 1:3). The date is the first of Nisan, the first month of the Jewish year, two weeks before Passover (see Exod 12:6). Mordecai, one of the two main characters, is introduced with a four-member genealogy that associates him with Saul, son of Kish (1 Sam 9:1). This relationship will prove significant. Mordecai

105

dragons advanced, both poised for combat. They uttered a mighty cry, ⁶and at their cry every nation prepared for war, to fight against the nation of the just. ⁷It was a dark and gloomy day. Tribulation and distress, evil and great confusion, lay upon the earth. ⁸The whole nation of the just was shaken with fear at the evils to come upon them, and they expected to perish. ⁹Then they cried out to God, and from their crying there arose, as though from a tiny spring, a mighty river, a flood of water. ¹⁰The light of the sun broke forth; the lowly were exalted and they devoured the boastful.

¹¹Having seen this dream and what God intended to do, Mordecai awoke. He kept it in mind, and tried in every way, until night, to understand its meaning.

Mordecai Thwarts an Assassination. ¹²Mordecai lodged in the courtyard with Bigthan and Teresh, two eunuchs of the king who guarded the courtyard. ¹³He overheard them plotting, investigated their plans, and discovered that they were preparing to assassinate King Ahasuerus. So he informed the king about them. ¹⁴The king had the two eunuchs questioned and, upon their confession, put to death. ¹⁵Then the king had these things recorded; Mordecai, too, put them into writing. ¹⁶The king also appointed Mordecai to serve at the court, and rewarded him for his actions.

¹⁷Haman, however, son of Hammedatha, a Bougean, who was held in high honor by the king, sought to harm Mordecai and his people because of the two eunuchs of the king.

---

is an exile, supposedly part of the first deportation under Nebuchadnezzar (see 2 Kgs 24:10-12). The place is Susa in Persia.

Mordecai has a dream full of apocalyptic imagery: dragons, darkness, total war (A:4-11). The message of the dream is also typical of apocalyptic worldview: "the nation of the just" is threatened with mortal danger but God saves them. The beginning of their salvation is symbolized by a mighty river that rises from a tiny spring. Mordecai cannot understand the dream; neither can we. It will be explained at the end of the story in addition F.

A:12-17 Mordecai thwarts an assassination

Mordecai's service to the king extends to saving his life. The consequence of his action is twofold: the king gives him a court appointment and Haman becomes his mortal enemy. Was Haman in on the plot? In any case, he is already portrayed as a villain. Both the king and Mordecai write down an account. These events lead to the major action of the story.

II. Esther Becomes Queen

1 The Banquet of Ahasuerus. ¹During the reign of Ahasuerus—the same Ahasuerus who ruled over a hundred and twenty-seven provinces from India to Ethiopia— ²while he was occupying the royal throne in the royal precinct of Susa, ³in the third year of his reign, he gave a feast for all his officials and ministers: the Persian and Median army officers, the nobles, and the governors of the provinces. ⁴For as many as a hundred and eighty days, he displayed the glorious riches of his kingdom and the resplendent wealth of his royal estate.

⁵At the end of this time the king gave a feast of seven days in the garden court of the royal palace for all the people, great and small, who were in the royal precinct of Susa. ⁶There were white cotton draperies and violet hangings, held by cords of fine crimson linen from silver rings on marble pillars. Gold and silver couches were on a mosaic pavement, which was of porphyry, marble, mother-of-pearl, and colored stones. ⁷Drinks were served in a variety of golden cups, and the royal wine flowed freely, as befitted the king's liberality. ⁸By ordinance of the king the drinking was unstinted, for he had instructed all the stewards of his household to comply with the good pleasure of everyone. ⁹Queen Vashti also gave a feast for the women in the royal palace of King Ahasuerus.

ESTHER BECOMES QUEEN

Esther 1:1–2:23

1:1-9 The banquet of Ahasuerus

The Hebrew version of the story also opens with significant information concerning the situation and themes of the book. The king is again identified by name and a description of his power is given. While it is true that the empire of Xerxes stretched from India to Ethiopia, the number of governmental divisions (satrapies) is usually given as about 30, not 120. The court is in Susa, the winter capital. The Greek historian Xenophon describes the unbearable heat of Susa in the summer. Other royal cities were Babylon, Ecbatana, and Persepolis. The time is the third year of the king's reign, thus a year after the events of addition A. The setting is a lavish royal banquet. The exaggeration that characterizes the whole book is evident here. All the important people of the whole realm are present for half a year (180 days). The king displays the extraordinary wealth of his palace and kingdom. The furnishings and the table service are lush! The Greek historian Herodotus reports on the extravagance of Persian drinking bouts, and this festivity is no exception. By the king's order everyone is to be given as much to drink as he desires.

Refusal of Vashti. ¹⁰On the seventh day, when the king was merry with wine, he instructed Mehuman, Biztha, Harbona, Bigtha, Abagtha, Zethar, and Carkas, the seven eunuchs who attended King Ahasuerus, ¹¹to bring Queen Vashti into his presence wearing the royal crown, that he might display her beauty to the populace and the officials, for she was lovely to behold. ¹²But Queen Vashti refused to come at the royal order issued through the eunuchs. At this the king's wrath flared up, and he burned with fury. ¹³He conferred with the sages who understood the times, because the king's business was conducted in general consultation with lawyers and jurists. ¹⁴He summoned Carshena, Shethar, Admatha, Tarshish, Meres, Marsena, and Memucan, the seven Persian and Median officials who were in the king's personal service and held first rank in the realm, ¹⁵and asked them, "What is to be done by law with Queen Vashti for disobeying the order of King Ahasuerus issued through the eunuchs?"

¹⁶In the presence of the king and of the officials, Memucan answered: "Queen Vashti has not wronged the king alone, but all the officials and the populace throughout the provinces of King Ahasuerus. ¹⁷For the queen's conduct will become known to all the women, and they will look with disdain upon their husbands when it is reported, 'King Ahasuerus commanded that Queen Vashti be ushered into his presence, but she would not come.' ¹⁸This very day the Persian and Median noblewomen who hear of the queen's conduct will recount it to all the royal officials, and disdain and rancor will abound. ¹⁹If it please the king, let an irrevocable royal decree be issued by him and inscribed among the laws of the Persians and Medes, forbidding Vashti to come into the presence of King Ahasuerus and authorizing the king to give her royal dignity to one more worthy than she. ²⁰Thus, when the decree that the king will issue is published throughout his realm, vast as it is, all wives will honor

Actually three banquets are described in this chapter: the 180-day banquet for all the prominent people of the kingdom (1:3-4); the seven-day banquet for the citizens of the royal district of Susa (1:5); and the banquet for the women given by the queen (1:9). The first banquet raises the question: "Who is minding the kingdom while all these officials are partying?" The third banquet makes it clear that the participants in the king's banquet are all men. It is also worth noting that the Hebrew word for banquet, *mishteh*, is derived from the word meaning "drink."

1:10-22 Refusal of Vashti

The first crisis emerges at the end of the king's second banquet. He already showed off all his glorious wealth; now, happily drunk, he wants to show off the beauty of his queen. Vashti is to come in all her finery, wearing the royal crown. He sends seven eunuchs to bring her from her banquet to his. The eunuchs are literally the middlemen who pass freely from the men's

their husbands, from the greatest to the least."

²¹This proposal pleased the king and the officials, and the king acted on the advice of Memucan. ²²He sent letters to all the royal provinces, to each province in its own script and to each people in its own language, to the effect that every man should be lord in his own home.

2 The Search for a New Queen. ¹After this, when King Ahasuerus' wrath had cooled, he thought over what Vashti had

area of the court to the women's. But Vashti will not come! Does she refuse simply because she will not demean herself (and him) by appearing before a roomful of drunken men? Is she too busy with her own party? The narrator does not reveal the reason.

The consequence, however, is clear. The king is furious. The rest of the scene reveals the character of the king and of his advisors (1:13-22). The king does not know what to do, so he confers with his lawyers and advisors. Several times throughout the story this king will not know what to do. One of his major advisors escalates the problem to the whole kingdom: Since Vashti has disobeyed the king, all the women of the province will disobey their husbands (1:17)! Vashti is banished from the king's presence (perhaps to her delight?) and one "better than she" will be chosen. (This raises the question of how Esther will be "better": more compliant, more beautiful?) The king is persuaded to issue an irrevocable decree that all wives will honor their husbands! A place is now opened for Esther to become queen. The decree is sent by the efficient postal service of the Persians (1:22). Throughout the book local problems will escalate to a national level. More irrevocable decrees will appear with sweeping demands on the population, and this amazing postal service will be used again.

In Memucan's suggestion concerning the deposing of Vashti, he says that the royal dignity will be taken from her and given to a neighbor who is better than she (1:19). The phrase echoes what Samuel says to Saul in the controversy over Agag (1 Sam 15:28; see commentary on 3:1-4).

Several elements indicate the comic and farcical nature of this story: the exaggeration, the impossible decree, the playing with numbers. On the seventh day of the banquet seven eunuchs are sent to bring the queen; when she refuses, the king consults seven advisors. Seven is the number for completion. The king's response to his wife's disobedience—sending a decree that all wives shall obey—is ironic to say the least. The pervasive exaggeration makes the Persian court an object of ridicule.

2:1-15 The search for a new queen

The king has a dilemma; he remembers Vashti and what happened but, because of the irrevocable decree, he has no solution (2:1). This king needs

done and what had been decreed against her. ²Then the king's personal attendants suggested: "Let beautiful young virgins be sought for the king. ³Let the king appoint emissaries in all the provinces of his realm to gather all beautiful young virgins into the harem in the royal precinct of Susa. Under the care of the royal eunuch Hegai, guardian of the women, let cosmetics be given them. ⁴Then the young woman who pleases the king shall reign in place of Vashti." This suggestion pleased the king, and he acted accordingly.

⁵There was in the royal precinct of Susa a certain Jew named Mordecai, son of Jair, son of Shimei, son of Kish, a Benjaminite, ⁶who had been exiled from Jerusalem with the captives taken with Jeconiah, king of Judah, whom Nebuchadnezzar, king of Babylon, had deported. ⁷He became foster father to his cousin Hadassah, that is, Esther, when she lost both father and mother. The young woman was beautifully formed and lovely to behold. On the death of her father and mother, Mordecai adopted her as his own daughter.

⁸When the king's order and decree had been proclaimed and many young women brought together to the royal precinct of Susa under the care of Hegai, Esther also was brought in to the royal palace under the care of Hegai, guardian of the women. ⁹The young woman pleased him and won his favor. So he promptly furnished her with cosmetics and provisions. Then choosing seven maids for her from the royal palace, he transferred both her and her maids to the best place in the harem. ¹⁰Esther did not reveal her nationality or family, for Mordecai had commanded her not to do so.

¹¹Day by day Mordecai would walk about in front of the court of the harem

---

advice for all his decisions! His servants suggest a roundup (what else could it be called?) of *all* the beautiful young virgins of the kingdom to find a woman "better than" Vashti (2:2-4). Many stories of such gatherings of women to please a potentate exist; perhaps the most familiar is found in the *Arabian Nights*. The fictional nature of this story is again indicated since by law Persian kings had to choose their queens from specific noble families.

The flow of the story is interrupted by the introduction of "Mordecai the Jew" (2:5-7; see A:1-3) The wording is virtually identical to the introduction of Saul in 1 Samuel 9:1; the ancestry of Mordecai also links him to Saul. The impossibility of his deportation in 597 B.C. is one of many indications that this is not a historical narrative. Xerxes began to reign in 485 B.C., so Mordecai would now be over one hundred and Esther would be in her sixties. The mention of the deportation in 597 rather than the one in 587, however, indicates that Mordecai belonged to a noble family (compare 2 Kgs 24:14-16 with 25:11-12). Esther is also introduced here (2:7). The only details are that she is orphaned and beautiful. The names Mordecai and

to learn how Esther was faring and what was to become of her.

[12]After the twelve months' preparation decreed for the women, each one went in turn to visit King Ahasuerus. During this period of beautifying treatment, six months were spent with oil of myrrh, and the other six months with perfumes and cosmetics. [13]Then, when each one was to visit the king, she was allowed to take with her from the harem to the royal palace whatever she chose. [14]She would go in the evening and return in the morning to a second harem under the care of the royal eunuch Shaashgaz, guardian of the concubines. She could not return to the king unless he was pleased with her and had her summoned by name. [15]As for Esther, daughter of Abihail and adopted daughter of his nephew Mordecai, when her turn came to visit the king, she did not ask for anything but what the royal eunuch Hegai, guardian of the women, suggested. And she won the admiration of all who saw her.

Ahasuerus Chooses Esther. [16]Esther was led to King Ahasuerus in his palace in the tenth month, Tebeth, in the seventh year of his reign. [17]The king loved Esther more than all other women, and of all the virgins she won his favor and good will. So he placed the royal crown on her head and made her queen in place of Vashti. [18]Then the king gave a great feast in honor of Esther to all his officials and servants, granting a holiday to the provinces and bestowing gifts with royal generosity.

Esther may be from the Mesopotamian gods Marduk and Ishtar. Each of them probably also has a Jewish name (see Dan 1:7) although only Esther's is given: Hadassah, meaning "myrtle."

The process of preparing the gathered virgins for the king's enjoyment is thorough and complex (2:8-15): a year of massages with aromatic oils and instructions regarding cosmetics and perfumes. Already Esther stands out: she gains the favor of Hegai (2:9) and of everyone else (2:15), presumably even the other young women! In one respect she is certainly "better" than Vashti: she is almost too compliant! She obeys Mordecai and does not reveal her Jewishness; she relies solely on Hegai's advice regarding what she should take with her for her night with the king.

2:16-18 Ahasuerus chooses Esther

Esther is taken to the king in the seventh year of his reign (another seven!), thus four years after Vashti's banishment. She not only pleases him and gains his favor, she wins his love. The word "love" to describe the relationship between a man and a woman appears only here (2:17). Ahasuerus crowns her as Vashti's replacement (with the crown Vashti was supposed to wear? see 1:11) and holds yet another great banquet.

Mordecai Thwarts an Assassination
[19]As was said, from the time the virgins had been brought together, and while Mordecai was passing his time at the king's gate, [20]Esther had not revealed her family or nationality, because Mordecai had told her not to; and Esther continued to follow Mordecai's instructions, just as she had when she was being brought up by him. [21]During the time that Mordecai spent at the king's gate, Bigthan and Teresh, two of the royal eunuchs who guarded the entrance, became angry and plotted to assassinate King Ahasuerus. [22]When the plot became known to Mordecai, he told Queen Esther, who in turn informed the king in Mordecai's name. [23]The matter was investigated and verified, and both of them were impaled on stakes. This was written in the annals in the king's presence.

III. Haman's Plot Against the Jews

3 Mordecai Refuses to Honor Haman. [1]After these events King Ahasuerus promoted Haman, son of Hammedatha the Agagite, to high rank, seating him above all his fellow officials. [2]All the king's servants who were at the royal gate would kneel and bow down to Haman, for that is what the king had ordered in his regard. Mordecai, however, would not kneel and bow down. [3]The king's servants who were at the royal gate said to Mordecai, "Why do you disobey the king's order?" [4]When

---

2:19-23 Mordecai thwarts an assassination

But all is not well in the kingdom. Mordecai, who may be at the gate because he holds an official position (see commentary on Ruth 4:1), discovers a plot to assassinate the king (see A:12-15). He sends word to the king through Esther and the plotters are executed in a manner common in Persia. Questions arise: Why must Esther not reveal her Jewish origins? Is there a fear of anti-Jewish sentiment? Why does Esther's association with Mordecai not give away the secret? Why is Mordecai not rewarded? The plot demands that these not be answered here. Esther must not be known as a Jew; otherwise Haman's villainy would not be possible. Mordecai's reward must wait until it exposes Haman's ambition.

HAMAN'S PLOT AGAINST THE JEWS

Esther 3:1-15; B:1-7

3:1-4 Mordecai refuses to honor Haman

After Mordecai saves the king, the reader expects him to be raised to a high position. Instead another man, Haman, is promoted. This promotion precipitates the crisis: Mordecai will not bow down to Haman. Why? The text does not reveal the reason, but several possibilities have been proposed: (1) Mordecai is arrogant; (2) he will bow to no one except God; (3) Mordecai

"The king loved Esther more than all other women . . ." (Esth 2:17).

they had reminded him day after day and he would not listen to them, they informed Haman, to see whether Mordecai's explanation would prevail, since he had told them that he was a Jew.

Haman's Reprisal. [5]When Haman observed that Mordecai would not kneel and bow down to him, he was filled with anger. [6]But he thought it was beneath him to attack only Mordecai. Since they had told Haman of Mordecai's nationality, he sought to destroy all the Jews, Mordecai's people, throughout the realm of King Ahasuerus. [7]In the first month, Nisan, in the twelfth year of King Ahasuerus, the *pur*, or lot, was cast in Haman's presence to determine the day and the month for the destruction of Mordecai's people on a single day, and the lot fell on the thirteenth day of the twelfth month, Adar.

Decree Against the Jews. [8]Then Haman said to King Ahasuerus: "Dispersed among the nations throughout the provinces of your kingdom, there is a certain people living apart. Their laws differ from those of every other people and they do not obey the laws of the king; so it is not proper for the king to tolerate them. [9]If it please the king, let a decree be issued to destroy them; and I will deliver to the procurators ten thousand silver talents for deposit in the royal treasury." [10]The king took the signet ring from his hand and gave it to Haman, son of Hammedatha the Agagite, the enemy of the Jews. [11]The king said to Haman, "The silver is yours, as well as the people, to do with as you please."

[12]So the royal scribes were summoned on the thirteenth day of the first month, and they wrote, at the dictation

---

will not bow to Haman because he is an Agagite; or (4) he refuses because Haman was part of the plot to assassinate Ahasuerus. The first two suggestions are not likely. Nowhere else in the story is Mordecai portrayed as arrogant; even when he saves the king's life he is self-effacing. Mordecai must already be in the habit of bowing to the king; otherwise he would have been noticed before this. However, compare C:7! The other two suggestions are more plausible. The Amalekites have been under a curse since they refused to let the Israelites pass through on their way to the Promised Land (Deut 25:17-19; see Exod 17:14). Saul, son of Kish, lost his throne because he failed to wipe out the Amalekites and kill Agag, their king (1 Sam 15:20-26). Mordecai is identified as a Benjaminite like Saul and a descendant of Kish. So it is no surprise that there would be mortal hatred between Haman and Mordecai. If the Greek additions are taken into consideration, there is enmity between them because Mordecai foiled the assassination plot (see A:17).

3:5-7 Haman's reprisal

Haman apparently does not notice Mordecai's refusal to bow until the other officials bring it to his attention (3:4). Then, just as Ahasuerus was

of Haman, an order to the royal satraps, the governors of every province, and the officials of every people, to each province in its own script and to each people in its own language. It was written in the name of King Ahasuerus and sealed with the royal signet ring. ¹³Letters were sent by couriers to all the royal provinces, to destroy, kill and annihilate all the Jews, young and old, including women and children in one day, the thirteenth day of the twelfth month, Adar, and to seize their goods as spoil.

---

enraged at Vashti's refusal, Haman is filled with anger. Ahasuerus responds to Vashti by issuing a decree regarding *all* women. Haman now plans a decree regarding *all* Jews (3:6). But whereas the response of Ahasuerus seemed ridiculous, Haman's plan is murderous.

Haman has lots cast, presumably to determine the most propitious date for the annihilation of the Jews. Verse 7, possibly a later insertion in the text, provides two critical bits of information. The "lot" is called *pur* from the Babylonian word *puru*. This provides an explanation of the name for the feast that the Jews will establish to celebrate their deliverance: Purim. The day on which the lot fell, the thirteenth of Adar, establishes the date for the proposed annihilation but will actually determine the date for the celebration (see 9:24-28).

3:8-15 Decree against the Jews

Just as Memucan proposed a solution to Ahasuerus regarding Vashti, Haman proposes a solution to the king regarding the slight to his own honor. The solution, however, is cleverly disguised so it seems that it is the king whose honor is being injured. He describes an unnamed people who are (1) dispersed throughout the kingdom but (2) distinct because of their own laws and customs. Then he accuses them of (3) refusing to obey the king's laws (3:8). The accusation is equivalent to treason. Haman begins with the truth, but his subtle move to untruth plants unwarranted suspicion in the king's mind. Haman concludes that the king must not tolerate these people but should have them destroyed (3:9). But before the king can respond, Haman offers ten thousand silver talents! This amount represents about two-thirds of the gross national product of Persia! It would seem that Haman is working for his own interests, not those of the king! It may also be true that the money convinces the king better than the argument does. The king authorizes Haman to do what he wishes with the people and hands over the signet ring to seal the decree in the king's name (3:10; see Joseph in Gen 41:42). Ahasuerus seems to refuse the money, but this may simply be Middle Eastern bargaining—saying "no" while accepting payment (3:11).

B ¹This is a copy of the letter:
"The great King Ahasuerus writes to the satraps of the hundred and twenty-seven provinces from India to Ethiopia, and the governors subordinate to them, as follows: ²When I came to rule many peoples and to hold sway over the whole world, not being carried away by a sense of my own authority but always acting fairly and with mildness, I determined to provide for my subjects a life of lasting tranquility; and, by making my kingdom civilized and safe for travel to its farthest borders, to restore the peace desired by all people. ³When I consulted my counselors as to how this might be accomplished, Haman, who excels among us in discretion, who is outstanding for constant good will and steadfast loyalty, and who has gained a place in the kingdom second only to me, ⁴brought it to our attention that, mixed among all the nations throughout the world, there is one people of ill will, which by its laws is opposed to every other people and continually disregards the decrees of kings, so that the unity of empire blamelessly designed by us cannot be established.

⁵"Having noted, therefore, that this nation, and it alone, is continually at variance with all people, lives by divergent and alien laws, is inimical to our government, and does all the harm it can to undermine the stability of the kingdom, ⁶we hereby decree that all those who are indicated to you in the letters of Haman, who is in charge of the administration and is a second father to us, shall, together with their wives and children, be utterly destroyed by the swords of their enemies, without any pity or mercy, on the fourteenth day of the twelfth month, Adar, of the current year;

The letters, dictated to scribes by Haman and sealed with the signet ring, are sent throughout the kingdom by the efficient Persian postal service (3:12-15). The summary is brutal: "to destroy, kill, and annihilate *all* the Jews, young and old, including women and children" (emphasis added). There is to be no mercy. *All* the people of the realm are to be prepared for that set day (3:14). The final sentence reveals the heartlessness of the king and Haman, who sit down to drink while the city of Susa is thrown into confusion (3:15). Greek historians say that the Persians either made or reconsidered decrees while they were drunk. The city of Susa refers to the city outside the royal precinct proper. Does the confusion indicate that the citizens are shocked at this command to slaughter their neighbors?

B:1-7 A copy of the letter

In the Septuagint a supposed copy of the letter interrupts the chapter between verses 13 and 14. (Compare the letters in Ezra 4:11-22; 7:11-26.) This addition, in contrast to addition A, was almost certainly written in Greek, not translated from an earlier Hebrew text. Ahasuerus is called the "great King," a title of Xerxes (see Introduction). The king is presented as

[7]so that when these people, whose present ill will is of long standing, have gone down into Hades by a violent death on a single day, they may leave our government completely stable and undisturbed for the future."

(CHAPTER 3)

[14]A copy of the decree to be promulgated as law in every province was published to all the peoples, that they might be prepared for that day. [15]The couriers set out in haste at the king's command; meanwhile, the decree was promulgated in the royal precinct of Susa. The king and Haman then sat down to drink, but the city of Susa was thrown into confusion.

IV. Esther and Mordecai Plead for Help

4 **Mordecai Exhorts Esther.** [1]When Mordecai learned all that was happening, he tore his garments, put on sackcloth and ashes, and went through the city crying out loudly and bitterly, [2]till he came before the royal gate, which no one clothed in sackcloth might enter. [3]Likewise in each of the provinces, wherever the king's decree and law reached, the Jews went into deep mourning, with fasting, weeping, and lament; most of them lay on sackcloth and ashes.

[4]Esther's maids and eunuchs came and told her. Overwhelmed with an-

acting in the best interests of the people. He is dependent particularly upon Haman, who "excels . . . in discretion" and is "outstanding for constant good will and steadfast loyalty" (B:3). This fulsome praise, which contradicts what is known of Haman from the rest of the story, reminds the reader that Haman himself dictated the letter! The description of the Jews (B:4-5) is even more damning than Haman's words to the king (3:8). The date set for their annihilation (without mercy) is the fourteenth of Adar, a day later than the date set in the Hebrew text. The author may have been confused by the fact that the celebration of Purim is a day later than the proposed slaughter.

ESTHER AND MORDECAI PLEAD FOR HELP

Esther 4:1–5a; C:1–D:16

4:1-17 Mordecai exhorts Esther

This chapter presents a dialogue between Mordecai and Esther through the intermediaries of her servants, especially the eunuch Hathach. Mordecai opens the conversation by not only exhibiting the traditional signs of mourning—torn garments, wearing of sackcloth and ashes—but by doing this at the very threshold of the royal gate. He is inches away from disobeying a royal law (4:2). His actions are reported to Esther, who is horrified. Is she afraid he will violate the law? Is she embarrassed by his behavior? In

guish, the queen sent garments for Mordecai to put on, so that he might take off his sackcloth; but he refused. ⁵Esther then summoned Hathach, one of the king's eunuchs whom he had placed at her service, and commanded him to find out what this action of Mordecai meant and the reason for it. ⁶So Hathach went out to Mordecai in the public square in front of the royal gate, ⁷and Mordecai recounted all that had happened to him, as well as the exact amount of silver Haman had promised to pay to the royal treasury for the slaughter of the Jews. ⁸He also gave him a copy of the written decree for their destruction that had been promulgated in Susa, to show and explain to Esther. Hathach was to instruct her to go to the king and to plead and intercede with him on behalf of her people.

⁹Hathach returned to Esther and told her what Mordecai had said. ¹⁰Then Esther replied to Hathach and gave him this message for Mordecai: ¹¹"All the servants of the king and the people of his provinces know that any man or woman who goes to the king in the inner court without being summoned is subject to the same law—death. Only if the king extends the golden scepter will such a person live. Now as for me, I have not been summoned to the king for thirty days."

¹²When Esther's words were reported to Mordecai, ¹³he had this reply brought to her: "Do not imagine that you are safe in the king's palace, you alone of all the Jews. ¹⁴Even if you now remain

---

any case, she, secluded in the harem, does not know of the decree against the Jews (4:5).

Esther first sends clothes, but Mordecai refuses (4:4). Then she sends Hathach to discover the reason for his risky actions. Hathach returns with detailed information: a copy of the decree and a report of the exact amount Haman promised to pay Ahasuerus (4:7-9). Mordecai also sends instructions to Esther to plead with the king for the Jews.

Hathach carries Esther's reply. The use of "know" is ironic. Mordecai learned ("came to know") all that was happening (4:1), but Esther did not know! She sent Hathach to find out (4:5). Now Esther tells Mordecai what everyone knows (4:11): to go to the king unbidden means certain death! Mordecai wins this interchange, however: "Who knows—perhaps it was for a time like this that you became queen?" (4:14)! It must be observed that through all this the servants (at least Hathach) know everything!

The Persian law that anyone who approaches the king without being summoned is subject to death is confirmed by the Greek historian Herodotus. But Herodotus also reports that it was possible to request an audience with the king. Somehow Esther had managed to get word to the king earlier concerning the assassination plot (2:22). The story is enhanced, however, by the queen risking her life.

silent, relief and deliverance will come to the Jews from another source; but you and your father's house will perish. Who knows—perhaps it was for a time like this that you became queen?"

15Esther sent back to Mordecai the response: 16"Go and assemble all the Jews who are in Susa; fast on my behalf, all of you, not eating or drinking night or day for three days. I and my maids will also fast in the same way. Thus prepared, I will go to the king, contrary to the law. If I perish, I perish!" 17Mordecai went away and did exactly as Esther had commanded.

C **Prayer of Mordecai.** 1Recalling all that the Lord had done, Mordecai prayed to the Lord 2and said: "Lord, Lord, King and Ruler of all, everything is in your power, and there is no one to oppose you when it is your will to save Israel. 3You made heaven and earth and every wonderful thing under heaven. 4You are Lord of all, and there is no one who can resist you, the Lord. 5You know

---

Mordecai points out two significant things: Esther will not escape death by keeping silent; if she does not respond, help will come from another source (4:13-14). She will not escape death because either Haman will find her out or the Jews who are saved will take vengeance on her as one of the perpetrators of the violence. This is a no-win situation. The other "source" from which help will come has often been interpreted as God (clearly so in the Septuagint, the Greek version of the Old Testament). God's help, however, may be indirect, perhaps through another palace coup. In any case, Mordecai has faith that the Jews will be delivered.

The crisis leads Esther to a transformation. She is faced with several life-threatening choices. She can choose to identify with the Persians and escape recognition as a Jew. She can choose to identify with the Jews and risk her life by going to the king to plead for them. She cannot, as Mordecai has pointed out, refuse to choose at all. At this point the woman who has obeyed every command given to her begins to issue commands. She commands Hathach (4:5) and Mordecai through Hathach (4:10). Now she sends Mordecai both her acceptance of his challenge and her instructions to him (4:16). She will risk her life, but everyone else must fast for three days on her behalf. (It is difficult not to see a request for prayer here!) Mordecai now obeys Esther, doing exactly what she has commanded (4:17). In later Jewish tradition there is observance of the Fast of Esther on the day before Purim.

C:1-11 ·Prayer of Mordecai

This addition from the Septuagint makes explicit what is never found in the Hebrew text of Esther: the main characters pray. Their prayer also reveals the theology and preoccupations of the Jewish people in the late second–early first century B.C.

119

all things. You know, Lord, that it was not out of insolence or arrogance or desire for glory that I acted thus in not bowing down to the arrogant Haman. ⁶I would have gladly kissed the soles of his feet for the salvation of Israel. ⁷But I acted as I did so as not to place the honor of a mortal above that of God. I will not bow down to anyone but you, my Lord. It is not out of arrogance that I am acting thus. ⁸And now, Lord God, King, God of Abraham, spare your people, for our enemies regard us with deadly envy and are bent upon destroying the inheritance that was yours from the beginning. ⁹Do not spurn your portion, which you redeemed for yourself out of the land of Egypt. ¹⁰Hear my prayer; have pity on your inheritance and turn our mourning into feasting, that we may live to sing praise to your name, Lord. Do not silence the mouths of those who praise you."

¹¹All Israel, too, cried out with all their strength, for death was staring them in the face.

Prayer of Esther. ¹²Queen Esther, seized with mortal anguish, fled to the Lord for refuge. ¹³Taking off her splendid garments, she put on garments of distress and mourning. In place of her precious ointments she covered her head with dung and ashes. She afflicted her body severely and in place of her festive adornments, her tangled hair covered her.

Mordecai not only calls the Jews to fast but also pleads with God to save them. The structure of his prayer is simple and traditional: praise of God (C:2-4), description/defense of his own situation (C:5-7), plea for God's help (C:8-10). Mordecai consistently uses the title "Lord" for God (eight times, plus two in the introduction), reflecting the privileged personal name of God revealed to Moses, Yhwh. He praises God's power in creation and in history and God's knowledge of all things. No one can resist God; no one knows all that God knows. In the middle section Mordecai defends his actions and gives a clear reason for his refusal to bow down to Haman: he will only bow down to God. (This contradicts the reality of the Hebrew story where Esther bows to the king in 8:3 and Mordecai surely does also.) In his plea to God Mordecai points out that it is in God's own interests to help the people: *your* people, *your* inheritance, *your* portion, redeemed for *yourself*, praise to *your* name. This line of persuasion is typical of biblical prayer (see Exod 32:11; Ps 74:1-2; 79:12-13).

C:12-30 Prayer of Esther

Esther too prays (compare Jdt 9). She identifies with her people (not the Persians) who are wearing sackcloth and ashes (see 4:3). She too cries to God as "Lord" (eight times, plus one in the introduction). She prays for her people and speaks a communal confession: we have sinned; we worshiped their gods (C:17-18). She also prays for herself. Twice she declares that she is alone and only God can help her (C:14, 25). She begs for courage (C:23,

¹⁴Then she prayed to the Lord, the God of Israel, saying: "My Lord, you alone are our King. Help me, who am alone and have no help but you, ¹⁵for I am taking my life in my hand. ¹⁶From birth, I have heard among my people that you, Lord, chose Israel from among all nations, and our ancestors from among all their forebears, as a lasting inheritance, and that you fulfilled all your promises to them. ¹⁷But now we have sinned in your sight, and you have delivered us into the hands of our enemies, ¹⁸because we worshiped their gods. You are just, O Lord. ¹⁹But now they are not satisfied with our bitter servitude, but have sworn an oath to their idols ²⁰to do away with the decree you have pronounced, to destroy your inheritance, to close the mouths of those who praise you, to extinguish the glory of your house and your altar, ²¹to open the mouths of the nations to acclaim their worthless gods, and to extol a mortal king forever.

²²"Lord, do not relinquish your scepter to those who are nothing. Do not let our foes gloat over our ruin, but turn their own counsel against them and make an example of the one who began this against us. ²³Be mindful of us, Lord. Make yourself known in the time of our distress and give me courage, King of gods and Ruler of every power. ²⁴Put in my mouth persuasive words in the presence of the lion, and turn his heart to hatred for our enemy, so that he and his co-conspirators may perish. ²⁵Save us by your power, and help me, who am alone and have no one but you, Lord.

²⁶"You know all things. You know that I hate the pomp of the lawless, and abhor the bed of the uncircumcised or of any foreigner. ²⁷You know that I am under constraint, that I abhor the sign of grandeur that rests on my head when I appear in public. I abhor it like a polluted rag, and do not wear it in private. ²⁸I, your servant, have never eaten at the table of Haman, nor have I graced the banquet of the king or drunk the wine of libations. ²⁹From the day I was brought here till now, your servant has had no joy except in you, Lord, God of Abraham. ³⁰O God, whose power is over all, hear the voice of those in despair. Save us from the power of the wicked, and deliver me from my fear."

---

30). Her description/defense of her own situation (C:26-29) illustrates the concerns of second-century Judaism: prohibition of marriage with non-Jews (see Neh 13:23-27) and dietary laws (see Dan 1:8-16). (Neither of these customs seems to be a problem in the Hebrew form of the story.) Esther's persuasion of God takes the form of remembering God's former acts of love and salvation (C:16) with the implication: "You saved us once; do it again!" (see Ps 77:11-13). She too declares that saving the people is in God's best interests: these enemies want to turn God's own people to praise of other gods and to lead them to honor a mortal king rather than the Lord who alone is their king (C:20). The enemy now seems to be all Gentiles and their false worship; there is only a suggestion of the threat of genocide. Her final sentence reveals the depth of her anguish.

DEsther Goes to Ahasuerus. [1]On the third day, ending her prayers, she took off her prayer garments and arrayed herself in her splendid attire. [2]In making her appearance, after invoking the all-seeing God and savior, she took with her two maids; [3]on the one she leaned gently for support, [4]while the other followed her, bearing her train. [5]She glowed with perfect beauty and her face was as joyous as it was lovely, though her heart was pounding with fear. [6]She passed through all the portals till she stood before the king, who was seated on his royal throne, clothed in full robes of state, and covered with gold and precious stones, so that he inspired great awe. [7]As he looked up in extreme anger, his features fiery and majestic, the queen staggered, turned pale and fainted, collapsing against the maid in front of her. [8]But God changed the king's anger to gentleness. In great anxiety he sprang from his throne, held her in his arms until she recovered, and comforted her with reassuring words. [9]"What is it, Esther?" he said to her. "I am your brother. Take courage! [10]You shall not die; this order of ours applies only to our subjects. [11]Come near!" [12]Raising the golden scepter, he touched her neck with it, embraced her, and said, "Speak to me."

[13]She replied: "I saw you, my lord, as an angel of God, and my heart was shaken by fear of your majesty. [14]For you are awesome, my lord, though your countenance is full of mercy." [15]As she said this, she fainted. [16]The king was shaken and all his attendants tried to revive her.

D:1-16; 5:1-5a Esther goes to Ahasuerus

The Hebrew text gives a straightforward account of Esther's approach to the king (5:1-2). She is literally clothed in royalty, the same royalty that Mordecai suggested was given her for just this purpose. With dignity she stands in the courtyard; she does not bow. She waits—for death or the king's invitation. He spies her and grants permission to approach by extending the royal scepter. The Greek addition D dramatizes the story, emphasizing Esther's courage in the face of mortal danger and God's rescue of her. God's presence is evident throughout the chapter. Esther has finished her long prayer but perhaps makes another short one (D:2). God changes the heart of the king from anger to gentleness when she approaches (D:8). Esther is both radiant and terrified (D:5). She goes all the way into the throne room, passing through "all the portals." Thus she has apparently defied the law, although the king later says that she is exempt. In her terror, she faints—twice (D:7, 15)! (But remember, she has been fasting for three days.) As for the king, his rage has been seen several times, but this is the first time that he appears truly regal. Interestingly, when he is majestic he is compassionate. Esther describes him as others described David: like an angel of God (D:13; see 2 Sam 14:17, 20). He describes himself simply as Esther's brother, a typical term for husband (D:9; see Song 4:9-12; Tob 7:11).

5 ¹[Now on the third day, Esther put on her royal garments and stood in the inner courtyard, looking toward the royal palace, while the king was seated on his royal throne in the audience chamber, facing the palace doorway. ²When he saw Queen Esther standing in the courtyard, she won his favor and he extended toward her the golden scepter he held. She came up to him, and touched the top of the scepter.]

³Then the king said to her, "What is it, Queen Esther? What is your request? Even if it is half of my kingdom, it shall be granted you." ⁴Esther replied, "If it please your majesty, come today with Haman to a banquet I have prepared." ⁵The king ordered, "Have Haman make haste to fulfill the wish of Esther."

V. Haman's Downfall

First Banquet of Esther. So the king went with Haman to the banquet Esther had prepared. ⁶During the drinking of the wine, the king said to Esther, "Whatever you ask for shall be granted, and whatever request you make shall be honored, even if it is for half my kingdom." ⁷Esther replied: "This is my petition and request: ⁸if I have found favor with the king and if it pleases your majesty to grant my petition and honor my request,

---

The reader expects Esther to plead for the lives of her people. The king has offered half his kingdom (5:3). Instead she invites the king and Haman to a banquet! Banquets have been critical occasions in this story. What will happen now? The delay contributes to the narrative tension. Ironically the king instructs Haman to make haste to fulfill whatever Esther wishes. Neither the king nor Haman knows what Esther really wants!

HAMAN'S DOWNFALL

Esther 5:5b–8:2

5:5b-8 First banquet of Esther

The question of Esther's request appears again at the banquet. Its importance is signaled by the threefold repetition of the double phrase: "ask/petition" and "request" (5:6, 7, 8; see 7:2-3). Again the king promises half the kingdom. Esther seems about to make her petition and request, but then she stops and instead invites the two guests to a second banquet. At the second banquet, she promises, she will reveal her petition and request. Why the second delay? It seems risky! Haman may discover her relationship to Mordecai; the king may change his mind about granting her request. Perhaps she wishes to increase the king's curiosity; perhaps his repeated offer of half the kingdom will shame him into granting her request whether he wants to or not. Perhaps she is securing the trap against Haman, lulling him into a proud security and suggesting to the king, ever so subtly, that

let the king come with Haman tomorrow to a banquet I will prepare; and tomorrow I will do as the king asks."

Haman's Plot Against Mordecai. ⁹That day Haman left happy and in good spirits. But when he saw that Mordecai at the royal gate did not rise, and showed no fear of him, he was filled with anger toward him. ¹⁰Haman restrained himself, however, and went home, where he summoned his friends and his wife Zeresh. ¹¹He recounted the greatness of his riches, the large number of his sons, and how the king had promoted him and placed him above the officials and royal servants. ¹²"Moreover," Haman added, "Queen Esther invited no one but me to come with the king to the banquet she prepared; again tomorrow I am to be her guest with the king. ¹³Yet none of this satisfies me as long as I continue to see the Jew Mordecai sitting at the royal gate." ¹⁴His wife Zeresh and all his friends said to him, "Have a stake set up, fifty cubits in height, and in the morning ask the king to have Mordecai impaled on it. Then go to the banquet with the king in good spirits." This suggestion pleased Haman, and he had the stake erected.

6 Mordecai's Reward from the King. ¹That night the king, unable to sleep,

---

she regards Haman as his equal. In any case, the reader's suspense is heightened.

5:9-14 Haman's plot against Mordecai

This section is framed by the image of Haman happy and in good spirits (5:9, 14). By contrast, Haman's mood is dark throughout the rest of the verses. Mordecai has great power over Haman rather than the reverse. Mordecai, now threatened with death, refuses to cower in Haman's presence. Not only does he not bow, he will not even stand (5:9)! Haman is enraged by this man who still sits at the gate! Like the king, however, Haman needs advice on how to deal with his rage. He calls his friends and his wife and begins by describing, not his troubles with Mordecai, but his own greatness (5:10-12). His wounded pride really needs comfort! When he finally admits that Mordecai is ruining his life, his wife and friends make an outlandish suggestion: Set up a stake seventy-five feet high (5:14). The stake will be higher than the palace. Haman will look as foolish as Ahasuerus did in chapter 1. The stake will be ready, so that Mordecai can be impaled on it as soon as Ahasuerus gives permission. Thus the king cannot change his mind! The end of the chapter is reminiscent of the end of chapter 3. After arranging for the execution, Haman can go to the party in good spirits.

6:1-13 Mordecai's reward from the king

In this chapter the comic nature of the story is stunningly evident. The irony (where the audience knows more than the characters) is rich and reversals of fortune are everywhere. The king cannot sleep. Why? Has he

asked that the chronicle of notable events be brought in. While this was being read to him, ²the passage occurred in which Mordecai reported Bigthan and Teresh, two of the royal eunuchs who guarded the entrance, for seeking to assassinate King Ahasuerus. ³The king asked, "What was done to honor and exalt Mordecai for this?" The king's attendants replied, "Nothing was done for him."

⁴"Who is in the court?" the king asked. Now Haman had entered the outer court of the king's palace to suggest to the king that Mordecai should be impaled on the stake he had raised for him. ⁵The king's attendants answered him, "Haman is waiting in the court." The king said, "Let him come in." ⁶When Haman entered, the king said to him, "What should be done for the man whom the king wishes to reward?" Now Haman thought to himself, "Whom would the king wish to honor more than me?" ⁷So he replied to the king: "For the man whom the king wishes to honor ⁸there should be brought the royal robe the king wore and the horse the king rode with the royal crest placed on its head. ⁹The robe and the horse should be given to one of the noblest of the king's officials, who must clothe the man the king wishes to reward, have him ride on

---

eaten or drunk too much at Esther's banquet? Is he plagued by curiosity regarding Esther's request? Is he nervous that Esther keeps honoring Haman? Perhaps there is no reason except narrative necessity—or the providence of God hidden in the events. Also, apparently by chance, the particular passage from the chronicles that is read to him is the story of Mordecai's saving his life (6:1-2). The king's desire to honor Mordecai (belatedly) sets up the rest of the chapter.

This king will do nothing without advice, so he asks for anyone who might be present in the court (6:4). It seems that Haman has not slept much either, for it must be very early in the morning. Both Haman and the king have something to ask. The king asks first. Just as Haman did not reveal the name of the people who were to be annihilated, so the king does not reveal the name of his intended honoree. This creates the opportunity for Haman to arrange his own undoing.

The key phrase, "the man whom the king wishes to honor," occurs four times. The king introduces it (6:6). Haman assumes it refers to himself (6:6). He uses it three times in his answer (6:7, 9 [twice]). Adele Berlin says that Haman is a "glutton for honor." His plan for honoring this favored person is excessive. It is similar to the pharaoh's honoring of Joseph (Gen 41:42-43), but here the honoree is wearing the king's own clothes and riding the king's own horse. It is unclear whether the horse is wearing the crown (what the Hebrew says) or whether this is the horse the king rode when he was crowned. Or perhaps Haman is so excited that his words are confused and

the horse in the public square of the city, and cry out before him, 'This is what is done for the man whom the king wishes to honor!'" [10]Then the king said to Haman: "Hurry! Take the robe and horse as you have proposed, and do this for the Jew Mordecai, who is sitting at the royal gate. Do not omit anything you proposed." [11]So Haman took the robe and horse, clothed Mordecai, had him ride in the public square of the city, and cried out before him, "This is what is done for the man whom the king wishes to honor!"

[12]Mordecai then returned to the royal gate, while Haman hurried home grieving, with his head covered. [13]When he told his wife Zeresh and all his friends everything that had happened to him, his advisers and his wife Zeresh said to him, "If Mordecai, before whom you are beginning to fall, is of Jewish ancestry, you will not prevail against him, but will surely be defeated by him."

Esther's Second Banquet. [14]While they were speaking with him, the king's eunuchs arrived and hurried Haman off to the banquet Esther had prepared.

7 [1]So the king and Haman went to the banquet with Queen Esther. [2]Again, on this second day, as they were drinking wine, the king said to Esther, "Whatever you ask, Queen Esther, shall be granted you. Whatever request you make, even

---

he means that he should wear the crown! Clearly Haman wants to be king! The Hebrew root *mlk*, meaning "to be king/royal," is repeated seven times in verses 8-9.

One can only imagine Haman's humiliation when he finds out the true honoree and then has to carry out what he himself has "proposed" (as the king reminds him twice; 6:10). The king identifies Mordecai as "the Jew." But it is unclear whether the king knows that the murderous decree is against the Jews, or whether he even remembers the decree.

Both Mordecai and Haman return to their places, but now Haman has all the signs of mourning as Mordecai did earlier (6:12). Again Haman repeats the events of the day to his wife and friends. This time, however, their advice is ominous: If (as is certainly true) Mordecai is a Jew, you will surely fall before him (6:13). How do they know this? Or are they speaking in the voice of the all-knowing narrator? They seem to be modeled on other non-Jews who announce such success (see Balaam in Num 23–24; Rahab in Josh 2:9-11; Achior in Jdt 5:5-21).

6:14–7:8 Esther's second banquet

Much has happened in the hours between Esther's first and second banquets. At this banquet Haman's fate will be sealed. Esther finally answers the king's question, using the two words he has consistently repeated. Literally she says, "Let my life be given to me according to my *petition* and my people according to my *request*." She has prefaced this with stock

for half the kingdom, shall be honored." ³Queen Esther replied: "If I have found favor with you, O king, and if it pleases your majesty, I ask that my life be spared, and I beg that you spare the lives of my people. ⁴For we have been sold, I and my people, to be destroyed, killed, and annihilated. If we were only to be sold into slavery I would remain silent, for then our distress would not have been worth troubling the king." ⁵King Ahasuerus said to Queen Esther, "Who and where is the man who has dared to do this?" ⁶Esther replied, "The enemy oppressing us is this wicked Haman." At this, Haman was seized with dread of the king and queen.

⁷The king left the banquet in anger and went into the garden of the palace, but Haman stayed to beg Queen Esther for his life, since he saw that the king had decided on his doom. ⁸When the king returned from the palace garden to the banquet hall, Haman had thrown himself on the couch on which Esther was reclining; and the king exclaimed, "Will he also violate the queen while she is with me in my own house!" Scarcely had the king spoken when the face of Haman was covered over.

---

phrases: "finding favor" and "pleasing your majesty." She has indeed found favor with everyone throughout the book (see 2:15, 17). She has subtly changed the phrase, "if I have found favor with the king" (see 5:8), to "if I have found favor with *you*, O king." She is gradually aligning herself with the king against Haman.

She explains her plea for her life and her people by quoting the decree authorizing the annihilation of the Jews: "destroyed, killed, and annihilated" (7:4; see 3:13). (Mordecai had sent her a copy of the decree; 4:8.) She contrasts two possible "sales" of herself and her people—to slavery or to death—and says that she would not have troubled the king if it were slavery. Here she appeals to his love of money. Presumably the king would have profited from their sale into slavery, but what can he gain from their deaths? She also indicates that the villain has usurped the king's power. No one can seize and sell people or property in a kingdom except the king. So Esther too has uncovered a plot against the king.

The action speeds up (7:5-8). Ahasuerus barks out the question: Who and where? Esther identifies Haman. The king leaves the room. Haman falls on Esther's couch (Persians reclined at meals) to beg for his life. The king returns and accuses him of attempted rape of the queen in his presence. Haman is a dead man.

Two questions arise concerning the king: Why did he leave? Why did he accuse Haman of rape when that must have been the last thing on Haman's mind? The king has a terrible dilemma. He has been confronted with a choice between his prime minister and his queen. Complicating the matter

Punishment of Haman. [9]Harbona, one of the eunuchs who attended the king, said, "At the house of Haman stands a stake fifty cubits high. Haman made it for Mordecai, who gave the report that benefited the king." The king answered, "Impale him on it." [10]So they impaled Haman on the stake he had set up for Mordecai, and the anger of the king abated.

8 [1]That day King Ahasuerus gave the house of Haman, enemy of the Jews, to Queen Esther; and Mordecai was admitted to the king's presence, for Esther had revealed his relationship to her. [2]The king removed his signet ring that he had taken away from Haman, and gave it to Mordecai; and Esther put Mordecai in charge of the house of Haman.

VI. The Jewish Victory and the Feast of Purim

The Second Royal Decree. [3]Esther again spoke to the king. She fell at his feet and tearfully implored him to revoke the harm done by Haman the Agagite and the plan he had devised against the Jews. [4]The king stretched forth the golden scepter to Esther. So she rose and, standing before him, [5]said: "If it seems good to the king and if I have found favor with him, if the thing seems right

is the fact that the king has approved the slaughter of the Jews, even though he may not have known or remembered which people were involved. Almost certainly he and Haman did not know that Esther was endangered by the decree. The appearance (however slight) of attempted rape gives the king a different reason to condemn Haman and thus gets him off the hook.

7:9–8:2 Punishment of Haman

Now the king needs advice on what to do. As always, someone else provides not only a suggestion but also another reason to condemn Haman. Haman has conspired against a benefactor of the king (Mordecai). The stake is already prepared for the execution of the king's enemy (now recognized to be Haman). The reversal of fate is finalized with the gift of Haman's house to Esther and his position, along with the signet ring, to Mordecai (8:1-2). It seems that the next line should be, "and everyone lived happily ever after." But the irrevocable decree against the Jews still stands.

JEWISH VICTORY AND THE FEAST OF PURIM

Esther 8:3–9:23; E:1-24

8:3-17 The second royal decree

The king may think he is finished, but Esther knows better. Just as Haman fell before her, pleading for his life, she falls pleading before the king. The same verb indicates that she is obeying Mordecai's injunction to

to the king and I am pleasing in his eyes, let a document be issued to revoke the letters that the schemer Haman, son of Hammedatha the Agagite, wrote for the destruction of the Jews in all the royal provinces. [6]For how can I witness the evil that is to befall my people, and how can I behold the destruction of my kindred?"

[7]King Ahasuerus then said to Queen Esther and to the Jew Mordecai: "Now that I have given Esther the house of Haman, and they have impaled him on the stake because he was going to attack the Jews, [8]you in turn may write in the king's name what you see fit concerning the Jews and seal the letter with the royal signet ring." For a decree written in the name of the king and sealed with the royal signet ring cannot be revoked.

[9]At that time, on the twenty-third day of the third month, Sivan, the royal scribes were summoned. Exactly as Mordecai dictated, they wrote to the Jews and to the satraps, governors, and officials of the hundred and twenty-seven provinces from India to Ethiopia: to each province in its own script and to each people in its own language, and to the Jews in their own script and language. [10]These letters, which he wrote in the name of King Ahasuerus and sealed with the royal signet ring, he sent by mounted couriers riding thoroughbred royal steeds. [11]In these letters the king authorized the Jews in each and every city to gather and defend their lives, to destroy, kill, and annihilate every armed group of any nation or province that

plead for the people (4:8). Haman is again identified as the Agagite, the age-old enemy of the Jews. The king indicates his willingness to listen by holding out the scepter.

Standing before him Esther begins with a four-part introduction (8:5). (Two or three clauses have previously been sufficient; see 5:4, 8; 7:3.) Two parts appeal to his love for her ("found favor" and "pleasing in his eyes"); two parts appeal to his good judgment in administering the kingdom ("good to the king" and "right"). Then she requests that the decree concerning the Jews be revoked. (By naming only Haman, she removes the king's responsibility for the decree.) The request is impossible, since royal decrees are irrevocable (1:19). The king responds by listing all the things he has already done—given her Haman's house and impaled him on a stake (8:7). Then, distancing himself even more from this unpleasant situation, he proposes an alternate solution: he gives to her and Mordecai authority to write whatever they wish in the king's name and to seal it with the royal seal. The decree is written at Mordecai's command, sealed, and sent by royal pony express (8:9-10; compare 3:12-13).

Authority shifts throughout this scene. Initially all authority belongs to the king (8:3-4). Esther pleads with him; he responds to Esther and Mordecai (8:7). The decree is then dictated by Mordecai alone (8:9). The first decree

might attack them, along with their wives and children, and to seize their goods as spoil [12]on a single day throughout the provinces of King Ahasuerus, the thirteenth day of the twelfth month, Adar.

E [1]The following is a copy of the letter: "The great King Ahasuerus to the governors of the provinces in the hundred and twenty-seven satrapies from India to Ethiopia, and to those who are loyal to our government: Greetings!

[2]"Many have become more ambitious the more they were showered with honors through the bountiful generosity of their patrons. [3]Not only do they seek to do harm to our subjects but, incapable of dealing with such greatness, they

---

regarding the Jews was dictated by the prime minister Haman (3:12); the second, dictated by the man who takes Haman's place, parallels the first.

The wording of this decree also echoes the former one: "to destroy, kill, and annihilate . . . along with their wives and children, and to seize their goods as spoil" (8:11; see 3:13). But the command is ambiguous. The Jews are authorized "to gather and defend their lives." Does this allow them a preemptive strike or only defensive action? The note about women and children is chilling. It comes from the "ban" (Hebrew *herem*) exercised in the Holy War tradition, where the Canaanite peoples were supposed to be completely exterminated (see Deut 7:1-2). The final event in Saul's collapse was his failure to kill Agag and all the Amalekites as required by the *herem* (1 Sam 15:3, 9-29).

The date of writing is puzzling: the twenty-third day of the third month (8:9). Haman's decree was issued on the thirteenth day of the first month (3:12). Mordecai's appeal to Esther, the fasting of the people, and the two banquets seem to follow in very close order, perhaps even in the space of a week. Why the delay before the second decree is issued? Is the date perhaps symbolic? There are seventy days between decrees. Is this intended to suggest the seventy-year exile? Another dating issue is also troubling. The three-day fast seems to be between the thirteenth and fifteenth of the first month, Nisan. Esther's first banquet (on the third day; 5:1) would then be the night after Passover (see Exod 12:2, 6). Symbolically this is highly significant as the day of deliverance. But why is there no mention anywhere of anyone celebrating Passover? Are all the Jews really fasting during Passover?

E:1-24 A copy of the letter

Another Greek addition is inserted here, a supposed copy of Mordecai's letter. This addition was almost certainly written in Greek (perhaps by the author of addition B) and at least a century after the Hebrew version of the story. In the letter Ahasuerus is portrayed as wise, generous, and concerned

even begin plotting against their own benefactors. ⁴Not only do they drive out gratitude from among humankind but, with the arrogant boastfulness of those to whom goodness has no meaning, they suppose they will escape the stern judgment of the all-seeing God.

⁵"Often, too, the fair speech of friends entrusted with the administration of affairs has induced many placed in authority to become accomplices in the shedding of innocent blood, and has involved them in irreparable calamities ⁶by deceiving with malicious slander the sincere good will of rulers. ⁷This can be verified in the ancient stories that have been handed down to us, but more fully when you consider the wicked deeds perpetrated in your midst by the pestilential influence of those undeserving of authority. ⁸We must provide for the future, so as to render the kingdom undisturbed and peaceful for all people, ⁹taking advantage of changing conditions and always deciding matters coming to our attention with equitable treatment.

¹⁰"For instance, Haman, son of Hammedatha, a Macedonian, certainly not of Persian blood, and very different from us in generosity, was hospitably received by us. ¹¹He benefited so much from the good will we have toward all peoples that he was proclaimed 'our father,' before whom everyone was to bow down; and he attained a position second only to the royal throne. ¹²But,

---

for the welfare of his people—and totally innocent of the previous decree authorizing the annihilation of the Jews. The king also seems to know Jewish belief: God is identified as "the Most High, the living God of majesty," and "the ruler of all" (E:16, 21). God is also given credit for the deliverance of the Jews in contrast to the Hebrew story in which God is not mentioned.

Haman is portrayed as thoroughly wicked. Most damning is his identification as a Macedonian (E:10). The Macedonians under Alexander the Great defeated the Persians under Darius II in 333 B.C. So Haman, who throughout the Hebrew version is identified as an Agagite and thus an enemy of Saul's descendants and all Jews, is here identified by another ethnic tag as the enemy of the Persians.

The people are instructed to "ignore" Haman's letter and to help the Jews (E:17-20). Is the king saying here that his letter really was not a royal decree, in spite of the royal seal? Does this second letter actually revoke the decree issued by Haman?

Two bits of information are anticipated: the death of Haman's sons (E:18), which in the Hebrew version happens in 9:7-10, and the establishment of Purim (E:21-22), which will be described in 9:17-23.

8:13-17 Public response

The mood changes with the return to the Hebrew story. The Jews are to be prepared to avenge themselves (8:13). Vengeance is a strange term here.

unable to control his arrogance, he strove to deprive us of kingdom and of life, [13]and by weaving intricate webs of deceit he demanded the destruction of Mordecai, our savior and constant benefactor, and of Esther, our blameless royal consort, together with their whole nation. [14]For by such measures he hoped to catch us defenseless and to transfer the rule of the Persians to the Macedonians. [15]But we find that the Jews, who were doomed to extinction by this archcriminal, are not evildoers, but rather are governed by very just laws [16]and are the children of the Most High, the living God of majesty, who has maintained the kingdom in a flourishing condition for us and for our forebears.

[17]"You will do well, then, to ignore the letter sent by Haman, son of Hammedatha, [18]for he who composed it has been impaled, together with his entire household, before the gates of Susa. Thus swiftly has God, who governs all, brought just punishment upon him.

[19]"You shall exhibit a copy of this letter publicly in every place to certify that the Jews may follow their own laws [20]and that you may help them on the day set for their ruin, the thirteenth day of the twelfth month, Adar, to defend themselves against those who attack them. [21]For God, the ruler of all, has turned that day from one of destruction of the chosen people into one of joy for them. [22]Therefore, you too must celebrate this memorable day among your designated feasts with all rejoicing, [23]so that both now and in the future it may be a celebration of deliverance for us and for Persians of good will, but for those who plot against us a reminder of destruction.

[24]"Every city and province without exception that does not observe this decree shall be ruthlessly destroyed with fire and sword, so that it will be left not merely untrodden by people, but even shunned by wild beasts and birds forever."

(CHAPTER 8)

[13]A copy of the letter to be promulgated as law in each and every province was published among all the peoples, so that the Jews might be prepared on that day to avenge themselves on their enemies. [14]Couriers mounted on royal steeds sped forth in haste at the king's order, and the decree was promulgated in the royal precinct of Susa.

[15]Mordecai left the king's presence clothed in a royal robe of violet and of white cotton, with a large crown of gold and a mantle of fine crimson linen. The city of Susa shouted with joy, [16]and for the Jews there was splendor and gladness, joy and triumph. [17]In each and

---

No one has yet done them any harm! In contrast to the actions of Haman after the first decree, Mordecai appears in public (8:15). He is regally clothed: Purple and crimson are expensive dyes and signs of royalty; the crown is also a sign of status, but it is called by a different Hebrew word to distinguish it from the king's crown. The response of the Jews everywhere to the new decree is great rejoicing. Especially in Susa, where there had been great confusion, there is now great joy.

every province and in each and every city, wherever the king's order arrived, there was merriment and joy, banqueting and feasting for the Jews. And many of the peoples of the land identified themselves as Jews, for fear of the Jews fell upon them.

9 **The Massacre Reversed.** ¹When the day arrived on which the order decreed by the king was to be carried out, the thirteenth day of the twelfth month, Adar, on which the enemies of the Jews had expected to overpower them, the situation was reversed: the Jews overpowered those who hated them. ²The Jews mustered in their cities throughout the provinces of King Ahasuerus to attack those who sought to do them harm, and no one could withstand them, for fear of them fell upon all the peoples. ³Moreover, all the officials of the provinces, the satraps, governors, and royal procurators supported the Jews out of fear of Mordecai; ⁴for Mordecai was powerful in the royal palace, and the report was spreading through all the provinces that he was continually growing in power.

⁵The Jews struck down all their enemies with the sword, killing and destroying them; they did to those who hated them as they pleased. ⁶In the royal precinct of Susa, the Jews killed and destroyed five hundred people. ⁷They also killed Parshandatha, Dalphon, Aspatha, ⁸Poratha, Adalia, Aridatha, ⁹Parmashta, Arisai, Aridai, and Vaizatha, ¹⁰the ten

---

Many people identified themselves as Jews (8:17). This can only mean that they sided with the Jews in preparing for the upcoming conflict. There has been a singular absence of overt religious practice throughout the book; thus it is unlikely that this sentence indicates religious conversion. The "fear of the Jews" should not be interpreted as a hidden reference to fear of the Lord. The Hebrew word (*pahad*) is not the ordinary word used in that phrase, and there is no reason to deny that the Persians are simply afraid of the Jews who have this newfound power!

9:1-17 The massacre reversed

The remaining chapters of the book of Esther represent several endings. This first ending brings to a head the theme of reversal, which is pervasive throughout the story. The thirteenth of Adar has arrived, the day on which the royal decree is to be carried out. But which decree—Haman's or Mordecai's? Apparently both! Those who expected to carry out the first are defeated by those empowered by the second (9:1). But there is no description of battles; it seems that the Jews meet little or no resistance. Somehow, however, they are enabled to make distinctions between "those who hated them" and those who supported them. Fear fills all the non-Jews, their enemies and their supporters: fear of the Jews as a people (because their fortunes have been so wonderfully reversed?) and fear of Mordecai, who grows ever more powerful (9:2-4). No Jewish casualties are reported. The

sons of Haman, son of Hammedatha, the foe of the Jews. However, they did not engage in plundering.

[11]On the same day, when the number of those killed in the royal precinct of Susa was reported to the king, [12]he said to Queen Esther: "In the royal precinct of Susa the Jews have killed and destroyed five hundred people, as well as the ten sons of Haman. What must they have done in the other royal provinces! You shall again be granted whatever you ask, and whatever you request shall be honored." [13]So Esther said, "If it pleases your majesty, let the Jews in Susa be permitted again tomorrow to act according to today's decree, and let the ten sons of Haman be impaled on stakes." [14]The king then gave an order that this be done, and the decree was published in Susa. So the ten sons of Haman were impaled, [15]and the Jews in Susa mustered again on the fourteenth of the month of Adar and killed three hundred people in Susa. However, they did not engage in plundering.

[16]The other Jews, who dwelt in the royal provinces, also mustered and defended themselves, and obtained rest from their enemies. They killed seventy-five thousand of those who hated them, but they did not engage in plunder. [17]This happened on the thirteenth day of the month of Adar.

---

other casualties are enormous, part of the exaggeration of the book: five hundred in the royal precinct of Susa, three hundred in the lower city of Susa, seventy-five thousand in the provinces (9:6, 15-16). The ten sons of Haman are also killed, those of whom he was so proud (9:7-10). Jewish tradition calls for reading the ten names in one breath, a reminder that even here the story is a comedy!

In the midst of recounting the slaughter, a little conversation between Esther and Ahasuerus appears (9:11-13). This vignette inspires laughter too. The king has only two things to say. First, he gleefully repeats the number killed in the royal precinct of Susa and wonders what has been achieved in the provinces. He has become the Jews' cheerleader! Second, he offers again to give Esther whatever she asks and whatever she requests (see 5:6; 7:2). Does he know no other question? Esther's request is surprising in its boldness: impale the corpses of Haman's ten sons and allow the people of the lower city of Susa to continue killing tomorrow (9:13). Haman's sons are thus publicly shamed as he was, and a reason is given for the custom of celebrating Purim on two different days.

Three times it is reported that the Jews did not engage in plunder (9:10, 15, 16), even though the decree permitted them to do so (see 8:11). This is the final echo of the story of Saul and Agag in 1 Samuel 15. Saul's undoing was the taking of plunder, thus disobeying the rule of Holy War. The Jews will not repeat his mistake.

The Feast of Purim. On the fourteenth of the month they rested, and made it a day of feasting and rejoicing.

[18]The Jews in Susa, however, mustered on the thirteenth and fourteenth of the month. But on the fifteenth they rested, and made it a day of joyful banqueting. [19]That is why the rural Jews, who dwell in villages, celebrate the fourteenth of the month of Adar as a day of joyful banqueting, a holiday on which they send food to one another.

[20]Mordecai recorded these events and sent letters to all the Jews, both near and far, in all the provinces of King Ahasuerus. [21]He ordered them to celebrate every year both the fourteenth and the fifteenth of the month of Adar [22]as the days on which the Jews obtained rest from their enemies and as the month which was turned for them from sorrow into joy, from mourning into celebration. They were to observe these days with joyful banqueting, sending food to one another and gifts to the poor. [23]The Jews adopted as a custom what they had begun doing and what Mordecai had written to them.

9:17b-23 The feast of Purim

The remaining verses of the chapter record the establishment of the feast of Purim. There are several explanations given for the feast. It must be well grounded since this feast is not found in the torah. Also, it seems that some festival was already celebrated and needed a foundation story (see 9:23). Finally, this festival was by custom celebrated on two different days, on the fourteenth in the rural areas and on the fifteenth in the walled cities. So a reason had to be given for the discrepancy. In Susa they fought an extra day (see 9:15-19).

What is being celebrated, according to the story, is not the battle but the "rest" from enemies (9:22). Thus the celebrations are set on the day *after* the battles (whether the fourteenth or the fifteenth). The way the festival is celebrated fits the story attached to it. This has been a story of banquets. So the celebration is characterized by much feasting, by giving presents—usually of food—to one another and also to the poor. The custom of including the poor in festivals is found throughout biblical tradition (see Deut 16:11; Neh 8:10-12; Tob 2:1-2).

VII. Epilogue: The Rise of Mordecai

Summary of the Story. [24]Haman, son of Hammedatha the Agagite, the foe of all the Jews, had planned to destroy them and had cast the *pur*, or lot, for the time of their defeat and destruction. [25]Yet, when the plot became known to the king, the king ordered in writing that the wicked plan Haman had devised against the Jews should instead be turned against Haman and that he and his sons should be impaled on stakes. [26]And so these days have been named Purim after the word *pur*.

Thus, because of all that was contained in this letter, and because of what they had witnessed and experienced in this event, [27]the Jews established and adopted as a custom for themselves, their descendants, and all who should join them, the perpetual obligation of celebrating these two days every year in the manner prescribed by this letter, and at the time appointed. [28]These days were to be commemorated and kept in every generation, by every clan, in every province, and in every city. These days of Purim were never to be neglected among the Jews, nor forgotten by their descendants.

Esther and Mordecai Act in Concert [29]Queen Esther, daughter of Abihail, and Mordecai the Jew, wrote to confirm with full authority this second letter about Purim, [30]and Mordecai sent documents concerning peace and security to all the Jews in the hundred and twenty-seven provinces of Ahasuerus' kingdom. [31]Thus were established, for their appointed time, these days of Purim which Mordecai the Jew and Queen Esther had designated for the Jews, just as they had previously enjoined upon themselves and upon their descendants the duty of fasting and supplication. [32]The command of Esther confirmed these prescriptions for Purim and was recorded in the book.

EPILOGUE: THE RISE OF MORDECAI

9:24–10:3; F:1-11

9:24-28 Summary of the story

The date, the reasons, and the way of celebrating have been determined. Now it remains to explain the name: Purim. The Babylonian term *pur* (the "lot" that Haman cast; see 3:7), which sounds like "Purim," is made the basis of the festival name (9:26).

9:29-32 Esther and Mordecai act in concert

All that remains is to establish the authority for the feast. Esther and Mordecai have worked in partnership to deliver the people from their enemies, so the introduction of the feast of Purim must be attributed to both. The letter attributed to Esther in verse 32 is credited to both Esther and Mordecai in verse 29. Mordecai's first letter (9:20-22) is attributed to both Mordecai and Esther in verse 31. Thus Purim is now firmly established.

10 The Rise of Mordecai Completed.

¹King Ahasuerus levied a tax on the land and on the islands of the sea. ²All the acts of his power and valor, as well as a detailed account of the greatness of Mordecai, whom the king promoted, are recorded in the chronicles of the kings of Media and Persia. ³The Jew Mordecai was next in rank to King Ahasuerus, in high standing among the Jews, popular with many of his kindred, seeking the good of his people and speaking out on behalf of the welfare of all its descendants.

F Mordecai's Dream Fulfilled.

¹Then Mordecai said: "This is the work of God. ²I recall the dream I had about these very things, and not a single detail has been left unfulfilled— ³the tiny spring that grew into a river, and there was light, and sun, and many waters. The river is Esther, whom the king married and made queen. ⁴The two dragons are myself and Haman. ⁵The nations are those who assembled to destroy the name of the Jews, ⁶but my people is Israel, who cried to God and was saved.

"The Lord saved his people and delivered us from all these evils. God worked signs and great wonders, such as have not occurred among the nations. ⁷For this purpose he arranged two lots: one for the people of God, the second for all the other nations. ⁸These two lots were fulfilled in the hour, the time, and the day of judgment before God and among all the nations. ⁹God remembered his people and rendered justice to his inheritance.

10:1-3 The rise of Mordecai completed

The end of the story returns to the beginning (see 1:1). Ahasuerus is again in complete control of the whole world (the land and the distant islands). But one important difference suggests that his kingdom is in better shape now, both for himself and for the Jews: Ahasuerus has Mordecai as his right-hand man! All these things are written down. In this story everything must be written down to be valid (see 1:22; 2:23; 3:12, 14; 4:8; 6:1-2; 8:8-13; 9:20, 23, 27, 29, 32). The book of Esther, after all, is known as *the* Scroll (see Introduction).

F:1-10 Mordecai's Dream Fulfilled

This Greek addition, an interpretation of the dream in addition A, also returns to the beginning. Throughout the Greek additions everything that has happened is attributed to God. The interpretation of the dream does not quite fit the story, however. It is not true that "not a single detail has been left unfulfilled," or at least unexplained (F:2). Esther is the river; is she also the tiny spring? Haman and Mordecai are the two dragons, but how is Mordecai like Haman, a dragon whose great cry inspires the nations to fight against the just (A:5-6)? What about the light and the sun (F:3)? Is this the splendid light that shone for the Jews when they heard Mordecai's decree (8:16)? The Greek interpreter does not tell us. A further discrepancy

[10]"Gathering together with joy and happiness before God, they shall celebrate these days on the fourteenth and fifteenth of the month Adar throughout all future generations of his people Israel."

Colophon [11]In the fourth year of the reign of Ptolemy and Cleopatra, Dosi-theus, who said he was a priest and Levite, and his son Ptolemy brought the present letter of Purim, saying that it was genuine and that Lysimachus, son of Ptolemy, of the community of Jerusalem, had translated it.

---

has to do with the question of "lots." God arranged two lots, one for God's people and one for others (F:7). The purpose of these lots is not the same as the single lot cast by Haman, although the mention of "the hour, the time, and the day" echoes that event (see 3:7). The plural "lots" may be an attempt to justify the apparent plural "Purim." (The "-im" ending signifies the plural in Hebrew.) In spite of all these differences, addition F wraps up the story one more time. God has saved his people (F:9)!

F:11 Colophon

A colophon is a later addition to a book, indicating critical information such as the author, the date, and the work's authenticity. This colophon does not clear up all the mysteries. Someone who claimed to be a priest and Levite identified this "letter of Purim" and its translator. Apparently the "letter of Purim" is the book of Esther in one of its versions, probably the Greek. Since there were several rulers named Ptolemy who had wives named Cleopatra, the date remains unclear—sometime between 116 and 48 B.C.

REVIEW AIDS AND DISCUSSION TOPICS

Song of Songs *(pages 9–30)*

1. What is the meaning of the title "Song of Songs"?

2. What is the role of Solomon in this and other wisdom books?

3. Why is "Song of Songs" included in the Scriptures? Does the presence of this book cause you to think of the Scriptures differently?

4. What are some of the metaphors the lovers use to address and describe each other? Come up with your own set of metaphors, engaging all the senses in your description.

5. What is the place of desire in the love between the woman and man? What does the book have to say about marriage?

6. How can we understand the role of the Daughters of Zion in the poem?

7. What does this book have to tell us about the role of erotic love in human experience?

Ruth *(pages 31–47)*

1. What does the book of Ruth tell us about the relationship between God and humanity?

2. Why is Ruth important to understanding the ancestry of David? The ancestry of Jesus?

3. This commentary analyzes the book of Ruth as literature. What are the important themes in this story?

4. Who are the important characters? Which ones do you like and why?

5. Can you think of parallels between this story and your own life or the life of someone you know?

Lamentations *(pages 48–70)*

1. How is the book of Lamentations used in the Jewish and Christian liturgical traditions?

2. What do you think might be the purpose of including laments in the Scriptures? What does their presence tell us about the relationship between humanity and God?

3. What is the image of Jerusalem ("Daughter Zion") developed in Lamentations 1?

4. How do the people in exile feel about the fall of Jerusalem? Where do they place the blame for the fall?

5. Compare the lament of chapter 3 with Psalms 42–43. What are the similarities?

6. Can you think of other figures in the Bible who make their complaints known to God? How does God respond? Have there been times in your own life when you have lamented to God? How might this book or lament psalms be helpful?

Ecclesiastes *(pages 71–102)*

1. Who is Qoheleth? What kind of person is he?

2. How do you understand the famous verse from this book: "Vanity of vanities, all is vanity!" How might you counter Qoheleth's arguments?

3. How do you understand the passage in chapter 3 about "an appointed time for everything"? How is this passage misunderstood or misinterpreted when it appears in other contexts?

4. How might the Christian belief in an afterlife affect our reading of Ecclesiastes?

5. Where do you find meaning in life? What role do possessions, accomplishments, work, recreation, and relationships play in your feelings about life?

6. Have you ever had the feelings that Qoheleth expresses in this book? If so, how did you respond to those feelings? Where did you find comfort or answers?

7. What is the meaning of life, ultimately, for Qoheleth? Given his understanding of life, what is the role of seeking wisdom instead of folly?

Esther *(pages 103–38)*

1. Describe Esther's situation. What strikes you as unusual about this story compared to others you have read in the Bible? What are the Greek elements of this story?

2. What is the difference between the Greek and Hebrew versions of the story? What is the difficulty of including only the Hebrew version in some translations of the Bible?

3. What characters are you drawn to in this story? Why?

4. On the feast of Purim, the story of Esther is dramatized. How would you tell the story in the context of a feast? Identify significant scenes and possible lines for a brief play based on the story.

5. What are the parts of Esther's prayer in addition C? Compare this prayer to the prayer in Judith 9.

6. Why do you think Esther has two banquets instead of one?

7. What is the role of God in the action and outcome of this story?

INDEX OF CITATIONS FROM THE
CATECHISM OF THE CATHOLIC CHURCH

The arabic number(s) following the citation refer(s) to the paragraph number(s) in the *Catechism of the Catholic Church*. The asterisk following a paragraph number indicates that the citation has been paraphrased.

Song of Songs		Lamentations		12:1	1007
1:7	2709	5:21	1432	12:7	1007
3:1-4	2709*				
8:6-7	1611	**Ecclesiastes**		**Esther**	
8:6	1040,* 1295*	3:20-21	703*	4:17b	269*

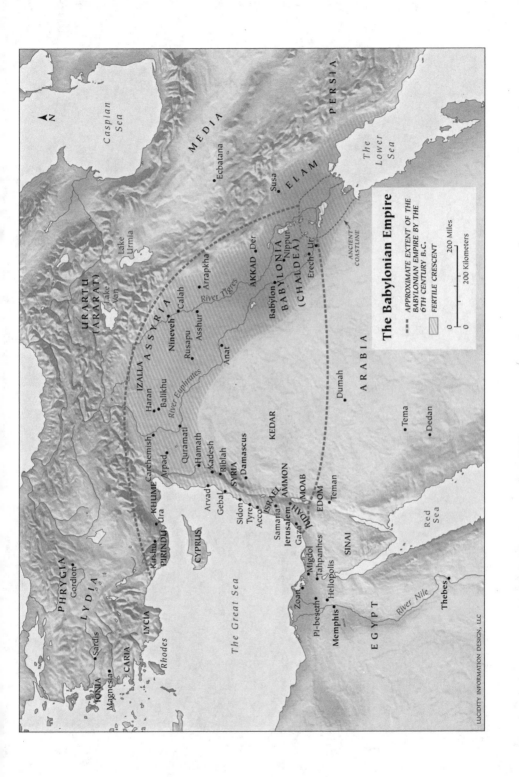

The Babylonian Empire

- - - APPROXIMATE EXTENT OF THE BABYLONIAN EMPIRE BY THE 6TH CENTURY B.C.
▨ FERTILE CRESCENT

0   200 Miles
0   200 Kilometers

LUCIDITY INFORMATION DESIGN, LLC

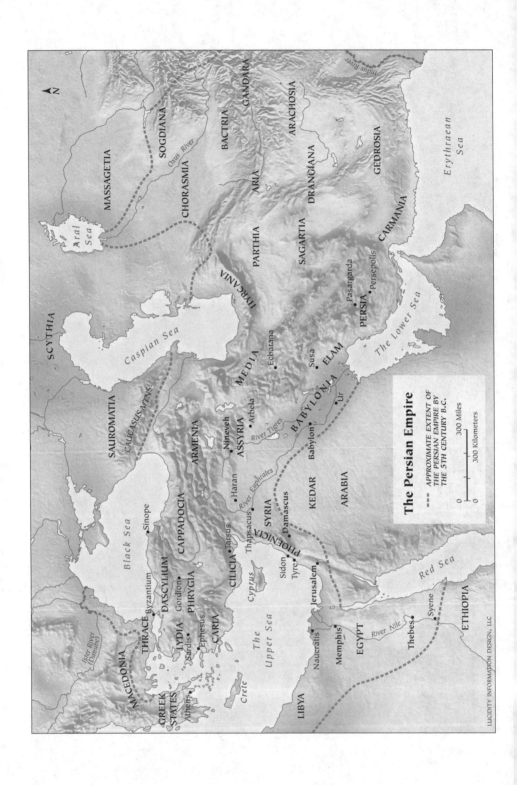

The Persian Empire

- ▬▬▬ APPROXIMATE EXTENT OF THE PERSIAN EMPIRE BY THE 5TH CENTURY B.C.

300 Miles

300 Kilometers

LUCIDITY INFORMATION DESIGN, LLC